21 LAWS OF LEADERSHIP IN THE BIBLE

LEARNING *to* LEAD *from the* MEN *and* WOMEN *of* SCRIPTURE

JOHN C. MAXWELL

THOMAS NELSON
Since 1798

21 Laws of Leadership in the Bible
© 2018 by John C. Maxwell

Published in Nashville, Tennessee, by Thomas Nelson. Thomas Nelson is a registered trademark of HarperCollins Christian Publishing, Inc.

Published in association with Yates & Yates, www.yates2.com

All Scripture quotations are taken from The Holy Bible, New International Version®, NIV®. Copyright © 1973, 1978, 1984, 2011 by Biblica, Inc.® Used by permission. All rights reserved worldwide. www.Zondervan.com. The "NIV" and "New International Version" are trademarks registered in the United States Patent and Trademark Office by Biblica, Inc.®

Thomas Nelson titles may be purchased in bulk for educational, business, fundraising, or sales promotional use. For information, please e-mail SpecialMarkets@ThomasNelson.com.

ISBN 978-0-310-08626-0

First Printing October 2018 / Printed in the United States of America

CONTENTS

ACKNOWLEDGMENTS

I want to say thank you to Charlie Wetzel and the rest of the team who assisted me with the formation and publication of this book. And to the people in my organizations who support it. You all add incredible value to me, which allows me to add value to others. Together, we're making a difference!

INTRODUCTION

Early in my career when I first began teaching people in church about leadership, they were often surprised. I was clearly young and inexperienced, yet the ideas I was able to convey seemed to be beyond what I should know. Later when I started writing about leadership, people gravitated to the message. And when I started writing and speaking to a more general audience, people often asked, "Where in the world did you learn all this?"

I was happy to let them in on a secret: everything I know about leadership I learned from the Bible.

Not only is the Bible the greatest book ever written, it is the greatest leadership book ever written. Everything you could ever want to learn about leadership—vision, purpose, thinking strategy, communication, attitude, encouragement, mentoring, follow-through—is all there. You just need to be open to what God wants to teach you. As it says in Isaiah 55:11,

> *My word that goes out from my mouth:*
>   *It will not return to me empty,*
> *but will accomplish what I desire*
>   *and achieve the purpose for which I sent it.*

God's word always fulfills his purpose. If you have felt a stirring to become a better leader or if someone has tapped your shoulder and asked you to lead, God will help you.

I am excited for you as you begin this journey of leadership development through the Word of God. I've chosen to organize this book around the 21 Laws of Leadership. You may be familiar with my book *The 21 Irrefutable Laws of Leadership: Follow Them and People Will Follow You*. If you are, the laws will be very familiar to you. If not, don't worry. I have included a brief excerpt from the book in each lesson to explain the law. But I've kept the focus of this workbook on Scripture. Each lesson contains three carefully selected biblical case studies—some positive, some negative—that reveal and illustrate the law. After you read each of these passages from the Bible, you will answer study questions that will prompt you to really dig into the Scripture and learn about leadership from it.

But this workbook isn't designed to be merely a theoretical exercise. It's meant to help you become a better leader. So following the passages and study questions, you will be directed to reflect on how you can apply the leadership lessons to your own life. You will also develop a specific action item to help you follow through and improve your leadership.

You can easily go through this workbook on your own and improve your leadership ability. But I want to encourage you to do this with a group. There's nothing like learning with other like-minded people who desire to grow and develop their leadership skills. To help you with this process, I've included group discussion questions at the end of each lesson.

My recommendation is that you gather a group of people to engage in the process together. Before you meet, each of you should complete the Study Questions, Leadership Insight and Reflection, and Taking Action sections on your own for that lesson. Then gather together as a group and answer the discussion questions. I believe you'll find you learn better and enjoy it more in a group.

May God bless you as you enjoy this journey.

THE LAW OF THE LID

Leadership Ability Determines a Person's Level of Effectiveness

DEFINITION OF THE LAW

Success is within the reach of just about everyone. While not every person can receive a 10 rating (on a success scale of 1 to 10), most people are capable of achieving some level of success or effectiveness in their lives. However, everyone eventually confronts a natural "lid" on their effectiveness, and that lid is leadership ability. The reality is that the level of your overall effectiveness can never rise higher than the level of your leadership ability. The higher the leadership ability, the greater the potential. The lower the leadership ability, the lower the impact.

Your leadership ability—for better or for worse—always affects your effectiveness and the potential impact of your organization. That's because as an individual, you can only succeed so much. There are just so many hours in a day for one person to work. Only when you partner with others and increase your effectiveness as a team can you move your personal success level past that lid.

Let's say your level of success is a 6 out of 10. That's pretty good. But like most people, you'd like to grow and raise that level. You have two choices: You could focus all your energy on increasing your personal effectiveness. You could work even harder and longer. And with all of that dedication, you might grow some. But eventually you would fill all of your time and exhaust yourself. A more efficient and fulfilling use of your time and energy would be to focus on growing as a leader.

When you raise your leadership ability—even without increasing your success dedication at all—you increase your success potential by a great deal. When you raise that lid, your influence will grow as a result. More people will want to follow you and work with you to achieve a goal. And more people dedicated to the vision means more time and energy devoted to its success. The more people you lead, and the more positive influence you have on them, the more you will achieve.

Leadership ability is also the lid on organizational effectiveness. If an organization's leadership is strong, its lid is high. But if it's not, then the organization is limited. That's why in times of trouble, organizations naturally look for new leadership. When the country is experiencing hard times, it elects a new president. When a company is losing money, it hires a new CEO. When a church is floundering, it searches for a new senior pastor. When a sports team keeps losing, it looks for a new head coach.

The more you want to achieve, the more you need leadership. The greater the impact you want to make, the greater your influence needs to be. Whatever you will accomplish is restricted by your ability to lead others. Grow as a leader, and you will multiply your—and your organization's—success. Leadership ability determines a person's level of effectiveness. That's the Law of the Lid.

CASE STUDIES

Read these case studies from the Bible and answer the study questions that follow.

① Aaron and Moses

Exodus 32:1–25

[1] When the people saw that Moses was so long in coming down from the mountain, they gathered around Aaron and said, "Come, make us gods who will go before us. As for this fellow Moses who brought us up out of Egypt, we don't know what has happened to him."

2 Aaron answered them, "Take off the gold earrings that your wives, your sons and your daughters are wearing, and bring them to me." 3 So all the people took off their earrings and brought them to Aaron. 4 He took what they handed him and made it into an idol cast in the shape of a calf, fashioning it with a tool. Then they said, "These are your gods, Israel, who brought you up out of Egypt."

5 When Aaron saw this, he built an altar in front of the calf and announced, "Tomorrow there will be a festival to the Lord." 6 So the next day the people rose early and sacrificed burnt offerings and presented fellowship offerings. Afterward they sat down to eat and drink and got up to indulge in revelry.

7 Then the Lord said to Moses, "Go down, because your people, whom you brought up out of Egypt, have become corrupt. 8 They have been quick to turn away from what I commanded them and have made themselves an idol cast in the shape of a calf. They have bowed down to it and sacrificed to it and have said, 'These are your gods, Israel, who brought you up out of Egypt.'

9 "I have seen these people," the Lord said to Moses, "and they are a stiff-necked people. 10 Now leave me alone so that my anger may burn against them and that I may destroy them. Then I will make you into a great nation."

11 But Moses sought the favor of the Lord his God. "Lord," he said, "why should your anger burn against your people, whom you brought out of Egypt with great power and a mighty hand? 12 Why should the Egyptians say, 'It was with evil intent that he brought them out, to kill them in the mountains and to wipe them off the face of the earth'? Turn from your fierce anger; relent and do not bring disaster on your people. 13 Remember your servants Abraham, Isaac and Israel, to whom you swore by your own self: 'I will make your descendants as numerous as the stars in the sky and I will give your descendants all this land I promised them, and it will be their inheritance forever.'" 14 Then the Lord relented and did not bring on his people the disaster he had threatened.

15 Moses turned and went down the mountain with the two tablets of the covenant law in his hands. They were inscribed on both sides, front and back. 16 The tablets were the work of God; the writing was the writing of God, engraved on the tablets.

17 When Joshua heard the noise of the people shouting, he said to Moses, "There is the sound of war in the camp."

¹⁸ Moses replied:

> *"It is not the sound of victory,*
> *it is not the sound of defeat;*
> *it is the sound of singing that I hear."*

¹⁹ When Moses approached the camp and saw the calf and the dancing, his anger burned and he threw the tablets out of his hands, breaking them to pieces at the foot of the mountain. ²⁰ And he took the calf the people had made and burned it in the fire; then he ground it to powder, scattered it on the water and made the Israelites drink it.

²¹ He said to Aaron, "What did these people do to you, that you led them into such great sin?"

²² "Do not be angry, my lord," Aaron answered. "You know how prone these people are to evil. ²³ They said to me, 'Make us gods who will go before us. As for this fellow Moses who brought us up out of Egypt, we don't know what has happened to him.' ²⁴ So I told them, 'Whoever has any gold jewelry, take it off.' Then they gave me the gold, and I threw it into the fire, and out came this calf!"

²⁵ Moses saw that the people were running wild and that Aaron had let them get out of control and so become a laughingstock to their enemies.

Study Questions

1. At the beginning of this story, who had greater influence on the other: Aaron or the people? Explain.

   _____

   _____

   _____

   _____

   _____

   _____

   _____

2. What does this say about Aaron's leadership? How did he handle his responsibilities? For what purpose did he use his influence?

_____

_____

_____

_____

3. How did Moses influence God in this passage? What did he say, and what was the outcome?

_____

_____

_____

_____

4. Describe Moses's responsibilities as a leader related to:

God _____

Aaron _____

Joshua _____

The People _____

For what purpose did he use his influence? How successful was he? What was the outcome?

_____

_____

_____

_____

2 David and Saul

1 Samuel 17:32–52

32 David said to Saul, "Let no one lose heart on account of this Philistine; your servant will go and fight him."

33 Saul replied, "You are not able to go out against this Philistine and fight him; you are only a young man, and he has been a warrior from his youth."

34 But David said to Saul, "Your servant has been keeping his father's sheep. When a lion or a bear came and carried off a sheep from the flock, 35 I went after it, struck it and rescued the sheep from its mouth. When it turned on me, I seized it by its hair, struck it and killed it. 36 Your servant has killed both the lion and the bear; this uncircumcised Philistine will be like one of them, because he has defied the armies of the living God. 37 The LORD who rescued me from the paw of the lion and the paw of the bear will rescue me from the hand of this Philistine."

Saul said to David, "Go, and the LORD be with you."

38 Then Saul dressed David in his own tunic. He put a coat of armor on him and a bronze helmet on his head. 39 David fastened on his sword over the tunic and tried walking around, because he was not used to them.

"I cannot go in these," he said to Saul, "because I am not used to them." So he took them off. 40 Then he took his staff in his hand, chose five smooth stones from the stream, put them in the pouch of his shepherd's bag and, with his sling in his hand, approached the Philistine.

41 Meanwhile, the Philistine, with his shield bearer in front of him, kept coming closer to David. 42 He looked David over and saw that he was little more than a boy, glowing with health and handsome, and he despised him. 43 He said to David, "Am I a dog, that you come at me with sticks?" And the Philistine cursed David by his gods. 44 "Come here," he said, "and I'll give your flesh to the birds and the wild animals!"

45 David said to the Philistine, "You come against me with sword and spear and javelin, but I come against you in the name of the LORD Almighty, the God of the armies of Israel, whom you have defied. 46 This day the LORD will deliver you into my hands, and I'll strike you down and cut off your head. This very day I will give the carcasses of the Philistine army to the birds and the wild animals, and the whole world will know that there is a God in Israel. 47 All those gathered here will know that it is not by sword or spear that the LORD saves; for the battle is the LORD's, and he will give all of you into our hands."

48 As the Philistine moved closer to attack him, David ran quickly toward the battle line to meet him. 49 Reaching into his bag and taking out a stone, he slung it and struck the Philistine on the forehead. The stone sank into his forehead, and he fell facedown on the ground.

⁵⁰ So David triumphed over the Philistine with a sling and a stone; without a sword in his hand he struck down the Philistine and killed him.

⁵¹ David ran and stood over him. He took hold of the Philistine's sword and drew it from the sheath. After he killed him, he cut off his head with the sword.

When the Philistines saw that their hero was dead, they turned and ran. ⁵² Then the men of Israel and Judah surged forward with a shout and pursued the Philistines to the entrance of Gath and to the gates of Ekron. Their dead were strewn along the Shaaraim road to Gath and Ekron.

Study Questions

1. Goliath taunted King Saul and the Israelites for forty days, and yet no champion went out to face him during that time. What does that say about Saul's leadership?

   _____

   _____

   _____

   _____

   _____

2. What gave David the courage to face the Philistine champion? How did that make him different from Saul?

   _____

   _____

   _____

   _____

   _____

3. How did David influence the two armies? How did they respond? What might have happened if David had not taken action?

   _____

   _____

   _____

   _____

   _____

4. What does this story say about the connection between action and influence?

_____

_____

_____

_____

_____

❸ Rehoboam and the People

1 Kings 12:1–20

¹ Rehoboam went to Shechem, for all Israel had gone there to make him king. ² When Jeroboam son of Nebat heard this (he was still in Egypt, where he had fled from King Solomon), he returned from Egypt. ³ So they sent for Jeroboam, and he and the whole assembly of Israel went to Rehoboam and said to him: ⁴ "Your father put a heavy yoke on us, but now lighten the harsh labor and the heavy yoke he put on us, and we will serve you."

⁵ Rehoboam answered, "Go away for three days and then come back to me." So the people went away.

⁶ Then King Rehoboam consulted the elders who had served his father Solomon during his lifetime. "How would you advise me to answer these people?" he asked.

⁷ They replied, "If today you will be a servant to these people and serve them and give them a favorable answer, they will always be your servants."

⁸ But Rehoboam rejected the advice the elders gave him and consulted the young men who had grown up with him and were serving him. ⁹ He asked them, "What is your advice? How should we answer these people who say to me, 'Lighten the yoke your father put on us'?"

¹⁰ The young men who had grown up with him replied, "These people have said to you, 'Your father put a heavy yoke on us, but make our yoke lighter.' Now tell them, 'My little finger is thicker than my father's waist. ¹¹ My father laid on you a heavy yoke; I will make it even heavier. My father scourged you with whips; I will scourge you with scorpions.'"

¹² Three days later Jeroboam and all the people returned to Rehoboam, as the king had said, "Come back to me in three days." ¹³ The king answered the people harshly. Rejecting the advice given him by the elders, ¹⁴ he followed the advice of the young men and said, "My father made your yoke heavy; I will make it even heavier. My father scourged you with whips; I will scourge you with scorpions." ¹⁵ So the king did not listen to the people, for this turn of events was from the LORD, to fulfill the word the LORD had spoken to Jeroboam son of Nebat through Ahijah the Shilonite.

¹⁶ When all Israel saw that the king refused to listen to them, they answered the king:

> *"What share do we have in David,*
> *what part in Jesse's son?*
> *To your tents, Israel!*
> *Look after your own house, David!"*

So the Israelites went home. ¹⁷ But as for the Israelites who were living in the towns of Judah, Rehoboam still ruled over them.

¹⁸ King Rehoboam sent out Adoniram, who was in charge of forced labor, but all Israel stoned him to death. King Rehoboam, however, managed to get into his chariot and escape to Jerusalem. ¹⁹ So Israel has been in rebellion against the house of David to this day.

²⁰ When all the Israelites heard that Jeroboam had returned, they sent and called him to the assembly and made him king over all Israel. Only the tribe of Judah remained loyal to the house of David.

Study Questions

1. What was Rehoboam's motivation for leadership? What were the motivations of the two groups who advised him?

_____

_____

_____

_____

_____

2. What was Rehoboam relying upon for his leadership to work? How effective was it?

_____

_____

_____

_____

_____

3. What might have happened if Rehoboam had listened to the elders? How might the history of Israel have been different as a result?

_____

_____

_____

_____

_____

4. David and Rehoboam were both young when they got their chance to lead in these passages. How were they similar? How were they different?

_____

_____

_____

_____

_____

LEADERSHIP INSIGHT AND REFLECTION

On a scale of 1 (low) to 10 (high), what leadership ratings would you give Aaron, Moses, David, Saul, and Rehoboam based on these passages? State the reason for your rating.

_____

_____

_____

_____

_____

By observing their leadership, what can you learn about your own leadership ability? How are your leadership limitations likely to affect your ability to accomplish your goals in life?

_____

_____

_____

_____

_____

_____

_____

_____

_____

TAKING ACTION

Keeping in mind that leadership ability determines a person's level of effectiveness, what can you do *immediately* to start becoming a better leader? Determine whether it is (check one) ...

- ❑ An attitude change
- ❑ A bad habit that needs to be broken
- ❑ A good habit that needs to be established
- ❑ An action to be taken with a person or people

What will you do?

_____

_____

_____

_____

_____

_____

_____

When will you do it?   Date: _____

Group Discussion Questions

1. In the past, how important was leadership to you personally? Has it been something you thought much about? Did you study it?

2. How important do you think it will be to you now? Explain.

3. Of the leaders you studied in the three Bible passages, who do you identify with the most? Why?

4. Who do you admire most? Why?

5. If you had to give yourself an overall leadership score from 1 (I can't lead anyone) to 10 (I could lead anyone, anywhere, on any level), what score would you give yourself? Why?

6. What was your greatest takeaway about leadership in this lesson?

7. What action do you believe God is asking you to take in your leadership as a result? When and how will you do it?

THE LAW OF INFLUENCE

The True Measure of Leadership Is Influence— Nothing More, Nothing Less

DEFINITION OF THE LAW

What is leadership? Many people believe it's a position. But if you watch the dynamics that occur between people in just about every aspect of life, you will see some people leading and others following, and you will notice that position and title often have little to do with who is really in charge. Still, those who have a leadership title often assume the role automatically makes them a leader. Others, who don't have an official leadership role, assume they can't possibly call themselves leaders. Neither group is correct. Leadership, by definition, is influence.

Leadership is not a title on a business card or a perk that can be offered with a promotion and a pay raise. True leadership cannot be awarded, appointed, or assigned. It comes only from influence, and that cannot be mandated. It must be earned. The only thing a title can buy is a little time—either to increase your level of influence with others or to undermine it.

Another widespread misunderstanding is that leading and managing are one and the same. Up until a few years ago, books that claimed to be on leadership were often really about management. The main difference between the two is that leadership is about influencing people to follow, while management focuses on maintaining systems and processes. Systems and processes can do only so much. To move people in a new direction, you need influence.

What about entrepreneurs? Many people assume that all entrepreneurs are leaders. But that's not always the case. Entrepreneurs are skilled at seeing opportunities and going after them. They see needs and understand how to meet them in a way that produces a profit. But some of them are not good with people. The most successful of those entrepreneurs choose to partner with someone else who is skilled at the people part of the equation.

In today's society, we tend to believe that expertise equals leadership. If so, then those who possess knowledge and intelligence would therefore be leaders. That isn't necessarily true. You can visit any major university and meet brilliant research scientists and philosophers whose ability to think is so high that it's off the charts, but whose ability to lead is so low that it doesn't even register on the charts. Neither IQ nor education necessarily equates to leadership.

Finally, another misconception is that anyone who is out in front of the crowd is a leader. But being first isn't always the same as leading. To be a leader, a person has to not only be out front but also have people intentionally coming behind him, following his lead, and acting on his vision. Being a trendsetter is not the same as being a leader.

I love the leadership proverb that says, "He who thinks he leads, but has no followers, is only taking a walk." If you can't influence people, then they will not follow you. And if people won't follow, you are not a leader. That's the Law of Influence. No matter what anybody else may tell you, remember that leadership is influence—nothing more, nothing less.

CASE STUDIES

Read these case studies from the Bible and answer the study questions that follow.

① Rahab's Influence

Joshua 2:1–24

1 Then Joshua son of Nun secretly sent two spies from Shittim. "Go, look over the land," he said, "especially Jericho." So they went and entered the house of a prostitute named Rahab and stayed there.

² *The king of Jericho was told, "Look, some of the Israelites have come here tonight to spy out the land." ³ So the king of Jericho sent this message to Rahab: "Bring out the men who came to you and entered your house, because they have come to spy out the whole land."*

⁴ *But the woman had taken the two men and hidden them. She said, "Yes, the men came to me, but I did not know where they had come from. ⁵ At dusk, when it was time to close the city gate, they left. I don't know which way they went. Go after them quickly. You may catch up with them." ⁶ (But she had taken them up to the roof and hidden them under the stalks of flax she had laid out on the roof.) ⁷ So the men set out in pursuit of the spies on the road that leads to the fords of the Jordan, and as soon as the pursuers had gone out, the gate was shut.*

⁸ *Before the spies lay down for the night, she went up on the roof ⁹ and said to them, "I know that the Lᴏʀᴅ has given you this land and that a great fear of you has fallen on us, so that all who live in this country are melting in fear because of you. ¹⁰ We have heard how the Lᴏʀᴅ dried up the water of the Red Sea for you when you came out of Egypt, and what you did to Sihon and Og, the two kings of the Amorites east of the Jordan, whom you completely destroyed. ¹¹ When we heard of it, our hearts melted in fear and everyone's courage failed because of you, for the Lᴏʀᴅ your God is God in heaven above and on the earth below.*

¹² *"Now then, please swear to me by the Lᴏʀᴅ that you will show kindness to my family, because I have shown kindness to you. Give me a sure sign ¹³ that you will spare the lives of my father and mother, my brothers and sisters, and all who belong to them—and that you will save us from death."*

¹⁴ *"Our lives for your lives!" the men assured her. "If you don't tell what we are doing, we will treat you kindly and faithfully when the Lᴏʀᴅ gives us the land."*

¹⁵ *So she let them down by a rope through the window, for the house she lived in was part of the city wall. ¹⁶ She said to them, "Go to the hills so the pursuers will not find you. Hide yourselves there three days until they return, and then go on your way."*

¹⁷ *Now the men had said to her, "This oath you made us swear will not be binding on us ¹⁸ unless, when we enter the land, you have tied this scarlet cord in the window through which you let us down, and unless you have brought your father and mother, your brothers and all your family into your house. ¹⁹ If any of them go outside your house into the street, their blood will be on*

their own heads; we will not be responsible. As for those who are in the house with you, their blood will be on our head if a hand is laid on them. ²⁰ *But if you tell what we are doing, we will be released from the oath you made us swear."*

²¹ *"Agreed," she replied. "Let it be as you say."*

So she sent them away, and they departed. And she tied the scarlet cord in the window.

²² *When they left, they went into the hills and stayed there three days, until the pursuers had searched all along the road and returned without finding them.* ²³ *Then the two men started back. They went down out of the hills, forded the river and came to Joshua son of Nun and told him everything that had happened to them.* ²⁴ *They said to Joshua, "The LORD has surely given the whole land into our hands; all the people are melting in fear because of us."*

Study Questions

1. What kind of formal leadership role do you think a prostitute like Rahab might have had in Jericho? Based on her interaction with Jericho's king and his officials, what kind of *real* influence do you think she had in the city? Explain.

_____

_____

_____

_____

2. Why do you think the spies chose Rahab to help them? Why did they trust her?

_____

_____

_____

_____

3. How were the spies influenced by Rahab? How were Joshua and the nation of Israel influenced by her?

_____

_____

_____

_____

4. What significance do you attribute to the fact that Rahab, a woman and a prostitute, is named in the story, but the two spies, trusted Israelite men, are not?

_____

_____

_____

_____

② Eli, His Sons, and Samuel

1 Samuel 2:12–26

¹² Eli's sons were scoundrels; they had no regard for the LORD. ¹³ Now it was the practice of the priests that, whenever any of the people offered a sacrifice, the priest's servant would come with a three-pronged fork in his hand while the meat was being boiled ¹⁴ and would plunge the fork into the pan or kettle or caldron or pot. Whatever the fork brought up the priest would take for himself. This is how they treated all the Israelites who came to Shiloh. ¹⁵ But even before the fat was burned, the priest's servant would come and say to the person who was sacrificing, "Give the priest some meat to roast; he won't accept boiled meat from you, but only raw."

¹⁶ If the person said to him, "Let the fat be burned first, and then take whatever you want," the servant would answer, "No, hand it over now; if you don't, I'll take it by force."

¹⁷ This sin of the young men was very great in the LORD's sight, for they were treating the LORD's offering with contempt.

¹⁸ But Samuel was ministering before the LORD—a boy wearing a linen ephod. ¹⁹ Each year his mother made him a little robe and took it to him when she went up with her husband to offer the annual sacrifice. ²⁰ Eli would bless Elkanah and his wife, saying, "May the LORD give you children by this woman to take the place of the one she prayed for and gave to the LORD." Then they would go home. ²¹ And the LORD was gracious to Hannah; she gave birth to three sons and two daughters. Meanwhile, the boy Samuel grew up in the presence of the LORD.

²² Now Eli, who was very old, heard about everything his sons were doing to all Israel and how they slept with the women who served at the entrance to the tent of meeting. ²³ So he said to them, "Why do you do such things? I hear from all the people about these wicked deeds of yours. ²⁴ No, my sons; the report I hear spreading among the Lᴏʀᴅ's people is not good. ²⁵ If one person sins against another, God may mediate for the offender; but if anyone sins against the Lᴏʀᴅ, who will intercede for them?" His sons, however, did not listen to their father's rebuke, for it was the Lᴏʀᴅ's will to put them to death.

²⁶ And the boy Samuel continued to grow in stature and in favor with the Lᴏʀᴅ and with people.

Study Questions

1. How would you describe the attitude and motives of Eli's sons when it came to leadership?

_____

_____

_____

_____

_____

2. How did Eli's sons go about getting what they wanted? Did they use influence, title, law, or some other means?

_____

_____

_____

_____

3. How would you describe Eli's attitude and motivation?

_____

_____

_____

_____

_____

4. Why wasn't Eli able to change the behavior of his sons, while Samuel, whom Eli also sought to influence, grew in favor with God and went in the right direction?

_____

_____

_____

_____

_____

_____

_____

❸ Paul: The Influential Prisoner

Acts 27:1–44

[1] When it was decided that we would sail for Italy, Paul and some other prisoners were handed over to a centurion named Julius, who belonged to the Imperial Regiment. [2] We boarded a ship from Adramyttium about to sail for ports along the coast of the province of Asia, and we put out to sea. Aristarchus, a Macedonian from Thessalonica, was with us.

[3] The next day we landed at Sidon; and Julius, in kindness to Paul, allowed him to go to his friends so they might provide for his needs. [4] From there we put out to sea again and passed to the lee of Cyprus because the winds were against us. [5] When we had sailed across the open sea off the coast of Cilicia and Pamphylia, we landed at Myra in Lycia. [6] There the centurion found an Alexandrian ship sailing for Italy and put us on board. [7] We made slow headway for many days and had difficulty arriving off Cnidus. When the wind did not allow us to hold our course, we sailed to the lee of Crete, opposite Salmone. [8] We moved along the coast with difficulty and came to a place called Fair Havens, near the town of Lasea.

[9] Much time had been lost, and sailing had already become dangerous because by now it was after the Day of Atonement. So Paul warned them, [10] "Men, I can see that our voyage is going to be disastrous and bring great loss to ship and cargo, and to our own lives also." [11] But the centurion,

instead of listening to what Paul said, followed the advice of the pilot and of the owner of the ship. 12 Since the harbor was unsuitable to winter in, the majority decided that we should sail on, hoping to reach Phoenix and winter there. This was a harbor in Crete, facing both southwest and northwest.

13 When a gentle south wind began to blow, they saw their opportunity; so they weighed anchor and sailed along the shore of Crete. 14 Before very long, a wind of hurricane force, called the Northeaster, swept down from the island. 15 The ship was caught by the storm and could not head into the wind; so we gave way to it and were driven along. 16 As we passed to the lee of a small island called Cauda, we were hardly able to make the lifeboat secure, 17 so the men hoisted it aboard. Then they passed ropes under the ship itself to hold it together. Because they were afraid they would run aground on the sandbars of Syrtis, they lowered the sea anchor and let the ship be driven along. 18 We took such a violent battering from the storm that the next day they began to throw the cargo overboard. 19 On the third day, they threw the ship's tackle overboard with their own hands. 20 When neither sun nor stars appeared for many days and the storm continued raging, we finally gave up all hope of being saved.

21 After they had gone a long time without food, Paul stood up before them and said: "Men, you should have taken my advice not to sail from Crete; then you would have spared yourselves this damage and loss. 22 But now I urge you to keep up your courage, because not one of you will be lost; only the ship will be destroyed. 23 Last night an angel of the God to whom I belong and whom I serve stood beside me24 and said, 'Do not be afraid, Paul. You must stand trial before Caesar; and God has graciously given you the lives of all who sail with you.' 25 So keep up your courage, men, for I have faith in God that it will happen just as he told me. 26 Nevertheless, we must run aground on some island."

27 On the fourteenth night we were still being driven across the Adriatic Sea, when about midnight the sailors sensed they were approaching land. 28 They took soundings and found that the water was a hundred and twenty feet deep. A short time later they took soundings again and found it was ninety feet deep. 29 Fearing that we would be dashed against the rocks, they dropped four anchors from the stern and prayed for daylight. 30 In an attempt to escape from the ship, the sailors let the lifeboat down into the sea, pretending they were going to lower some anchors from the bow.

31 Then Paul said to the centurion and the soldiers, "Unless these men stay with the ship, you cannot be saved." 32 So the soldiers cut the ropes that held the lifeboat and let it drift away.

33 Just before dawn Paul urged them all to eat. "For the last fourteen days," he said, "you have been in constant suspense and have gone without food—you haven't eaten anything. 34 Now I urge you to take some food. You need it to survive. Not one of you will lose a single hair from his head." 35 After he said this, he took some bread and gave thanks to God in front of them all. Then he broke it and began to eat. 36 They were all encouraged and ate some food themselves. 37 Altogether there were 276 of us on board. 38 When they had eaten as much as they wanted, they lightened the ship by throwing the grain into the sea.

39 When daylight came, they did not recognize the land, but they saw a bay with a sandy beach, where they decided to run the ship aground if they could. 40 Cutting loose the anchors, they left them in the sea and at the same time untied the ropes that held the rudders. Then they hoisted the foresail to the wind and made for the beach. 41 But the ship struck a sandbar and ran aground. The bow stuck fast and would not move, and the stern was broken to pieces by the pounding of the surf.

42 The soldiers planned to kill the prisoners to prevent any of them from swimming away and escaping. 43 But the centurion wanted to spare Paul's life and kept them from carrying out their plan. He ordered those who could swim to jump overboard first and get to land. 44 The rest were to get there on planks or on other pieces of the ship. In this way everyone reached land safely.

Study Questions

1. At the beginning of this story, who had the most influence? Why?

_____

_____

_____

_____

_____

_____

2. How did Paul's influence with the centurion, the soldiers, and the others change over the course of the story? Why did it change?

_____

_____

_____

_____

3. What was Paul's motivation for leading the people on the ship?

_____

_____

_____

_____

LEADERSHIP INSIGHT AND REFLECTION

In the three passages, who gained influence over time? Why? Who lost influence? Why?

_____

_____

_____

_____

_____

The people in these passages had various levels of formal authority. Eli, his sons, and Samuel possessed titles and positions. Rahab was a woman and a prostitute, which meant she had absolutely no standing in the ancient world. Paul, though a Roman citizen, was a prisoner whom the soldiers could have executed to keep from escaping. The centurion had a title and position. What do all these differences say about leadership?

_____

_____

_____

_____

_____

What do their stories say about who God uses to make a difference?

_____
_____
_____
_____
_____
_____
_____
_____
_____

TAKING ACTION

Keeping in mind that leadership is influence, describe where God is calling you to lead because you already have influence or because you could have influence. What are you prepared to commit to do with your influence starting today? Describe it in as much detail as you can.

_____
_____
_____
_____
_____
_____
_____
_____
_____
_____
_____
_____
_____
_____

GROUP DISCUSSION QUESTIONS

1. What do you think was the most difficult task for Rahab from the time the spies arrived in Jericho to the time the walls fell before the Israelites? Why?

2. The passage in 1 Samuel 2 says the sons of Eli were scoundrels. Obviously, you would be speculating, but why do you think they became that way?

3. How do you think Paul was able to keep his composure in the midst of the difficulties he and his shipmates were facing?

4. How did the various people in the stories handle power when they got it? How did each of them react when put in a tenuous or inferior position?

5. How do you react when you are put in power? In a tenuous position? Why?

6. What was your greatest takeaway about leadership and influence in this lesson?

7. What action do you believe God is asking you to take in your leadership as a result of this lesson? When and how will you do it?

THE LAW OF PROCESS

Leadership Develops Daily, Not in a Day

DEFINITION OF THE LAW

Are leaders born? Or made? Maybe the answer is "both." We're all born with certain natural abilities and gifts. And of course, some people are born with greater natural leadership gifts than others. Fortunately, the ability to lead is really a collection of skills, nearly all of which can be learned and improved. So while perhaps not everyone can become a *great* leader, anyone can become a *better* leader. But it's important to recognize that leadership has many facets: respect, experience, emotional strength, people skills, discipline, vision, momentum, timing. It's a complicated skill set, and many of the skills are intangible. They take time to develop. And that's where the Law of Process comes in. Leadership develops daily, not in a day.

Becoming a leader is a lot like investing successfully in the stock market. If your hope is to make a fortune in a day, you're probably going to be disappointed. Most of the successful investors are in it for the long haul. They add to their investments regularly, and those investments tend to compound over time.

Unfortunately, most people overestimate the importance of events and underestimate the power of processes. We want quick fixes. We want the big jackpot. We want the compounding effect that happens over fifty years, but we want it in fifty minutes. But there are no successful lottery winners or "day traders" in leadership development. What matters most is what you do day by day over the long haul.

That's why a process is so much more effective than a one-time event. Consider the difference between the two:

An Event	**A Process**
Encourages decisions	Encourages development
Motivates people	Matures people
Is a calendar issue	Is a culture issue
Challenges people	Changes people
Is easy	Is difficult

The secret of our success can be found in our daily agenda. What can you see when you look at a person's daily agenda? Priorities, passion, abilities, relationships, attitude, personal disciplines, vision, and influence. See what a person is doing every day, day after day, and you'll know who that person is and what he or she is becoming. And the learning process is ongoing, a result of self-discipline and perseverance. The goal each day must be to get a little better, to build on the previous day's progress.

If you want to be a leader, the good news is that you can do it. Everyone has the potential, but it isn't accomplished overnight. It requires perseverance. And you absolutely cannot ignore the Law of Process. Leadership doesn't develop in a day. It takes a lifetime.

CASE STUDIES

Read these case studies from the Bible and answer the study questions that follow.

❶ The Value of Joseph's Growth as a Leader

Acts 7:9–19

9 *"Because the patriarchs were jealous of Joseph, they sold him as a slave into Egypt. But God was with him* 10 *and rescued him from all his troubles. He*

gave Joseph wisdom and enabled him to gain the goodwill of Pharaoh king of Egypt. So Pharaoh made him ruler over Egypt and all his palace.

[11] "Then a famine struck all Egypt and Canaan, bringing great suffering, and our ancestors could not find food. [12] When Jacob heard that there was grain in Egypt, he sent our forefathers on their first visit. [13] On their second visit, Joseph told his brothers who he was, and Pharaoh learned about Joseph's family. [14] After this, Joseph sent for his father Jacob and his whole family, seventy-five in all. [15] Then Jacob went down to Egypt, where he and our ancestors died. [16] Their bodies were brought back to Shechem and placed in the tomb that Abraham had bought from the sons of Hamor at Shechem for a certain sum of money.

[17] "As the time drew near for God to fulfill his promise to Abraham, the number of our people in Egypt had greatly increased. [18] Then 'a new king, to whom Joseph meant nothing, came to power in Egypt.' [19] He dealt treacherously with our people and oppressed our ancestors."

Psalm 105:16–23

[16] [God] called down famine on the land
    and destroyed all their supplies of food;
[17] and he sent a man before them—
    Joseph, sold as a slave.
[18] They bruised his feet with shackles,
    his neck was put in irons,
[19] till what he foretold came to pass,
    till the word of the Lord proved him true.
[20] The king sent and released him,
    the ruler of peoples set him free.
[21] He made him master of his household,
    ruler over all he possessed,
[22] to instruct his princes as he pleased
    and teach his elders wisdom.
[23] Then Israel entered Egypt;
    Jacob resided as a foreigner in the land of Ham.

Study Questions

1. How do you think Joseph felt when his brothers, referred to as the patriarchs in the first passage, sold him into slavery and he was taken in chains to Egypt?

_____

_____

_____

_____

_____

_____

2. The Genesis story of Joseph recounts that as a teenager he had a dream in which his brothers and parents were bowing to him, the implication being that he would rule over them. When Joseph found himself a slave, what chances do you think he believed he had of becoming a leader?

_____

_____

_____

_____

_____

_____

3. For more than two decades, everywhere Joseph went as a slave—in the household of Pharaoh's captain of the guard, the prison, and then Pharaoh's court—he rose up in leadership. Why did God have Joseph go through this process? Why didn't God simply elevate Joseph immediately?

_____

_____

_____

_____

_____

_____

② Moses Couldn't Skip the Development Process

Exodus 2:5–15

⁵*Pharaoh's daughter went down to the Nile to bathe, and her attendants were walking along the riverbank. She saw the basket among the reeds and sent her female slave to get it.* ⁶*She opened it and saw the baby. He was crying, and she felt sorry for him. "This is one of the Hebrew babies," she said.*

⁷*Then his sister asked Pharaoh's daughter, "Shall I go and get one of the Hebrew women to nurse the baby for you?". . .* ¹⁰*When the child grew older, [the baby's mother] took him to Pharaoh's daughter and he became her son. She named him Moses, saying, "I drew him out of the water."*

¹¹*One day, after Moses had grown up, he went out to where his own people were and watched them at their hard labor. He saw an Egyptian beating a Hebrew, one of his own people.* ¹²*Looking this way and that and seeing no one, he killed the Egyptian and hid him in the sand.* ¹³*The next day he went out and saw two Hebrews fighting. He asked the one in the wrong, "Why are you hitting your fellow Hebrew?"*

¹⁴*The man said, "Who made you ruler and judge over us? Are you thinking of killing me as you killed the Egyptian?" Then Moses was afraid and thought, "What I did must have become known."*

¹⁵*When Pharaoh heard of this, he tried to kill Moses, but Moses fled from Pharaoh and went to live in Midian.*

Exodus 3:1–2, 7–12

¹*Now Moses was tending the flock of Jethro his father-in-law, the priest of Midian, and he led the flock to the far side of the wilderness and came to Horeb, the mountain of God.* ²*There the angel of the LORD appeared to him in flames of fire from within a bush. . . .*

⁷*The LORD said, "I have indeed seen the misery of my people in Egypt. I have heard them crying out because of their slave drivers, and I am concerned about their suffering.* ⁸*So I have come down to rescue them*

from the hand of the Egyptians and to bring them up out of that land into a good and spacious land, a land flowing with milk and honey—the home of the Canaanites, Hittites, Amorites, Perizzites, Hivites and Jebusites. ⁹ And now the cry of the Israelites has reached me, and I have seen the way the Egyptians are oppressing them. ¹⁰ So now, go. I am sending you to Pharaoh to bring my people the Israelites out of Egypt."

¹¹ But Moses said to God, "Who am I that I should go to Pharaoh and bring the Israelites out of Egypt?"

¹² And God said, "I will be with you."

Study Questions

1. Moses grew up as the son of Pharaoh's daughter. How do you think this might have shaped his view of leadership?

_____

_____

_____

_____

_____

_____

_____

2. Why do you think Moses killed the Egyptian who was arguing with the Hebrew? Why did he try to intervene with the two fighting Hebrews? What do you think Moses hoped to accomplish?

_____

_____

_____

_____

_____

_____

_____

_____

3. Moses spent many years in the desert of Midian. Some people speculate it could have been a many as forty, yet Scripture doesn't reveal much of what happened during that time. What do you believe Moses learned during that time? Could he have learned the same lessons while remaining in Egypt? Explain.

_____

_____

_____

_____

_____

_____

_____

_____

_____

_____

4. Why do you think Moses was reluctant to lead God's people out of Egypt?

_____

_____

_____

_____

_____

_____

_____

_____

3 It Took Time for Peter to Live Up to His Name

Matthew 16:15–19

[15] *"But what about you?" [Jesus] asked. "Who do you say I am?"*
    [16] *Simon Peter answered, "You are the Messiah, the Son of the living God."*
    [17] *Jesus replied, "Blessed are you, Simon son of Jonah, for this was not revealed to you by flesh and blood, but by my Father in heaven. [18] And I tell you that you are Peter, and on this rock I will build my church, and the gates of Hades will not overcome it. [19] I will give you the keys of the kingdom of*

heaven; *whatever you bind on earth will be bound in heaven, and whatever you loose on earth will be loosed in heaven."*

Matthew 26:69–75

⁶⁹ *Now Peter was sitting out in the courtyard, and a servant girl came to him. "You also were with Jesus of Galilee," she said.*

⁷⁰ *But he denied it before them all. "I don't know what you're talking about," he said.*

⁷¹ *Then he went out to the gateway, where another servant girl saw him and said to the people there, "This fellow was with Jesus of Nazareth."*

⁷² *He denied it again, with an oath: "I don't know the man!"*

⁷³ *After a little while, those standing there went up to Peter and said, "Surely you are one of them; your accent gives you away."*

⁷⁴ *Then he began to call down curses, and he swore to them, "I don't know the man!"*

Immediately a rooster crowed. ⁷⁵ *Then Peter remembered the word Jesus had spoken: "Before the rooster crows, you will disown me three times." And he went outside and wept bitterly.*

Acts 2:36–41

³⁶ *[Peter said,] "Therefore let all Israel be assured of this: God has made this Jesus, whom you crucified, both Lord and Messiah."*

³⁷ *When the people heard this, they were cut to the heart and said to Peter and the other apostles, "Brothers, what shall we do?"*

³⁸ *Peter replied, "Repent and be baptized, every one of you, in the name of Jesus Christ for the forgiveness of your sins. And you will receive the gift of the Holy Spirit.* ³⁹ *The promise is for you and your children and for all who are far off—for all whom the Lord our God will call."*

⁴⁰ *With many other words he warned them; and he pleaded with them, "Save yourselves from this corrupt generation."* ⁴¹ *Those who accepted his message were baptized, and about three thousand were added to their number that day.*

Study Questions

1. Why did Jesus give Simon the new name Peter, meaning "the rock"?

_____

_____

_____

_____

_____

2. What caused Peter to deny Jesus, even after the disciple had declared that he would never forsake his master?

_____

_____

_____

_____

_____

_____

3. How do you reconcile the difference between the rock who declared that Jesus is the Son of God with the person who crumbled under pressure and denied Jesus? What does it say about Peter's leadership?

_____

_____

_____

_____

_____

4. What changed between the time Peter denied knowing Jesus and the time Peter preached and thousands came to faith? How had Peter grown as a leader?

_____

_____

_____

_____

LEADERSHIP INSIGHT AND REFLECTION

How do you think Joseph, Moses, and Peter felt about having to wait before being entrusted with leadership? Explain.

_____

_____

_____

_____

_____

_____

_____

_____

What lessons do you believe God wanted Joseph, Moses, and Peter to learn before they were ready to receive their leadership responsibilities?

_____

_____

_____

_____

_____

_____

_____

_____

What do you believe God wants you to learn currently to prepare you for leadership or make you a better leader?

_____

_____

_____

_____

_____

_____

_____

_____

TAKING ACTION

Think about what God wants you to learn to become a better leader. It may be a lesson or skill. It may be a talent that needs to be developed. It may involve breaking bad habits or developing good ones. What can you do as a *daily practice* for the next thirty days to learn?

_____

_____

_____

_____

_____

_____

When is the *soonest* you can start?

_____

_____

_____

Write what you learn from the experience here:

_____

_____

_____

_____

_____

_____

_____

_____

_____

_____

_____

GROUP DISCUSSION QUESTIONS

1. How do you think Joseph felt and what kind of growth did he need at each of these stages of his life:

   - When he had the vision of ruling his family?
   - When he was first sold into slavery?
   - When he was learning to lead while a slave?
   - When Pharaoh put him in charge of Egypt?
   - When his brothers came to Egypt begging for food?
   - When his entire family was resettled in Egypt?

2. What role did God play in the leadership success of Joseph, Moses, and Peter? What is the basis of your answer?

3. When have you experienced an especially fulfilling or beneficial time of spiritual growth with God? What prompted it? How did you grow?

4. What is the greatest leadership learning experience you've ever had? What prompted it? How did you grow? How did you apply what you learned?

5. How do you know when it's time to focus on growing your leadership and when it's time to rely on God and take a leap of faith in your leadership?

6. What was your greatest takeaway about the process of leadership growth you gained from this lesson?

7. What action do you believe God is asking you to take in your leadership growth as a result of this lesson? When and how will you do it?

THE LAW OF NAVIGATION

Anyone Can Steer the Ship, but It Takes a Leader to Chart the Course

DEFINITION OF THE LAW

Imagine leaving on vacation with a destination in mind but no idea of how to get there. If the trip is short and not too complicated, you might be able to guess and stumble your way from here to there. But if the terrain is unknown, or the distance is uncertain, then you're just as likely to fumble your way right to the edge of a cliff. Good expedition leaders do more than declare the destination; they study the map and chart the course. They do more than control the direction in which they and their people travel. They see the whole trip in their minds before they leave the dock. That's the Law of Navigation. Nearly anyone can steer the ship, but it takes a leader to chart the course. Preparation is the key.

To prepare for the journey, effective navigators begin by drawing on past experiences. They take the time to look back and apply the lessons of other journeys to the one before them. This means learning not only from the times when they reached their destination but also from those when they came up short. In fact, the lessons from failures are usually much more useful in charting a successful course in the future.

After looking back at past experiences, good navigators examine the current conditions. They mark the map with their location, the destination, and every turn in between. Then they ponder the issues that could affect the journey, from tangible things like terrain, season, weather, team members, and supplies, to intangibles such as timing, morale, momentum, and culture. By figuring out the conditions, navigators can better predict the amount of effort, resources, and time the journey will take.

Once navigators examine the past and the present, they dig deeper by looking outside of themselves. They gather information from many sources. They study the journeys of those who have gone before. They consult experts and leaders from outside the organization who can mentor them. They listen to their team members to find out what's happening "in the trenches." By going beyond their own personal observations, they obtain a fuller picture of where they are and how to get where they need to go.

Finally, after learning everything they can, good navigators make sure their conclusions represent both faith and fact. Effective leaders have faith that they can take their people all the way. But they also strive to see the facts realistically. You can't minimize obstacles or rationalize about challenges and still lead effectively. If you don't go in with your eyes wide open, you're going to get blindsided.

Good preparation does more than help the leader create the map; it also conveys confidence and trust to followers. Lack of preparation has the opposite effect. In the end, it's not the size of the project that determines its acceptance, support, and success. It's the size of the leader. That's why I say that anyone can *steer* the ship, but it takes a leader to chart the course. Leaders who are good navigators are capable of taking their people just about anywhere.

CASE STUDIES

Read these case studies from the Bible and answer the study questions that follow.

❶ Joshua's Plan of Attack

Joshua 8:1–19, 28

¹ Then the LORD said to Joshua, "Do not be afraid; do not be discouraged. Take the whole army with you, and go up and attack Ai. For I have delivered into your

hands the king of Ai, his people, his city and his land. ² *You shall do to Ai and its king as you did to Jericho and its king, except that you may carry off their plunder and livestock for yourselves. Set an ambush behind the city."*

³ *So Joshua and the whole army moved out to attack Ai. He chose thirty thousand of his best fighting men and sent them out at night* ⁴ *with these orders: "Listen carefully. You are to set an ambush behind the city. Don't go very far from it. All of you be on the alert.* ⁵ *I and all those with me will advance on the city, and when the men come out against us, as they did before, we will flee from them.* ⁶ *They will pursue us until we have lured them away from the city, for they will say, 'They are running away from us as they did before.' So when we flee from them,* ⁷ *you are to rise up from ambush and take the city. The LORD your God will give it into your hand.* ⁸ *When you have taken the city, set it on fire. Do what the LORD has commanded. See to it; you have my orders."*

⁹ *Then Joshua sent them off, and they went to the place of ambush and lay in wait between Bethel and Ai, to the west of Ai—but Joshua spent that night with the people.*

¹⁰ *Early the next morning Joshua mustered his army, and he and the leaders of Israel marched before them to Ai.* ¹¹ *The entire force that was with him marched up and approached the city and arrived in front of it. They set up camp north of Ai, with the valley between them and the city.* ¹² *Joshua had taken about five thousand men and set them in ambush between Bethel and Ai, to the west of the city.* ¹³ *So the soldiers took up their positions—with the main camp to the north of the city and the ambush to the west of it. That night Joshua went into the valley.*

¹⁴ *When the king of Ai saw this, he and all the men of the city hurried out early in the morning to meet Israel in battle at a certain place overlooking the Arabah. But he did not know that an ambush had been set against him behind the city.* ¹⁵ *Joshua and all Israel let themselves be driven back before them, and they fled toward the wilderness.* ¹⁶ *All the men of Ai were called to pursue them, and they pursued Joshua and were lured away from the city.* ¹⁷ *Not a man remained in Ai or Bethel who did not go after Israel. They left the city open and went in pursuit of Israel.*

¹⁸ *Then the LORD said to Joshua, "Hold out toward Ai the javelin that is in your hand, for into your hand I will deliver the city." So Joshua held out toward the city the javelin that was in his hand.* ¹⁹ *As soon as he did this,*

the men in the ambush rose quickly from their position and rushed forward. They entered the city and captured it and quickly set it on fire. . . .

²⁸ So Joshua burned Ai and made it a permanent heap of ruins, a desolate place to this day.

Study Questions

1. The Israelites' first attempt to conquer Ai failed because one member of their camp had disobeyed God. How do you think this impacted Joshua's thinking as a leader?

_____

_____

_____

_____

_____

_____

2. How much of the strategy for conquering Ai was given by God, and how much was contributed by Joshua?

_____

_____

_____

_____

_____

3. Do you think the positive outcome of the battle would have happened no matter what? Or do you believe that if Joshua had demonstrated poor leadership, the victory could have been prevented? Explain.

_____

_____

_____

_____

_____

② Nehemiah Rallied His People to Rebuild and Defend

Nehemiah 4:7–23

7 But when Sanballat, Tobiah, the Arabs, the Ammonites and the people of Ashdod heard that the repairs to Jerusalem's walls had gone ahead and that the gaps were being closed, they were very angry. 8 They all plotted together to come and fight against Jerusalem and stir up trouble against it. 9 But we prayed to our God and posted a guard day and night to meet this threat.

10 Meanwhile, the people in Judah said, "The strength of the laborers is giving out, and there is so much rubble that we cannot rebuild the wall."

11 Also our enemies said, "Before they know it or see us, we will be right there among them and will kill them and put an end to the work."

12 Then the Jews who lived near them came and told us ten times over, "Wherever you turn, they will attack us."

13 Therefore I stationed some of the people behind the lowest points of the wall at the exposed places, posting them by families, with their swords, spears and bows. 14 After I looked things over, I stood up and said to the nobles, the officials and the rest of the people, "Don't be afraid of them. Remember the Lord, who is great and awesome, and fight for your families, your sons and your daughters, your wives and your homes."

15 When our enemies heard that we were aware of their plot and that God had frustrated it, we all returned to the wall, each to our own work.

16 From that day on, half of my men did the work, while the other half were equipped with spears, shields, bows and armor. The officers posted themselves behind all the people of Judah 17 who were building the wall. Those who carried materials did their work with one hand and held a weapon in the other, 18 and each of the builders wore his sword at his side as he worked. But the man who sounded the trumpet stayed with me.

19 Then I said to the nobles, the officials and the rest of the people, "The work is extensive and spread out, and we are widely separated from each other along the wall. 20 Wherever you hear the sound of the trumpet, join us there. Our God will fight for us!"

21 So we continued the work with half the men holding spears, from the first light of dawn till the stars came out. 22 At that time I also said to the

*people, "Have every man and his helper stay inside Jerusalem at night,
so they can serve us as guards by night and as workers by day." ²³ Neither I nor
my brothers nor my men nor the guards with me took off our clothes; each had
his weapon, even when he went for water.*

Study Questions

1. What obstacles and challenges did Nehemiah face in his effort to rebuild
   the wall around Jerusalem? List all of them, including any that were not
   mentioned explicitly in the passage but that you may discern by reading
   between the lines.

   _____

   _____

   _____

   _____

   _____

   _____

   _____

   _____

   _____

   _____

2. Examine the obstacles you listed. Beside each, write a word or phrase
   in the margin noting how Nehemiah solved it. What does his navigation
   of problems to accomplish each task tell you about how he led and
   solved problems?

   _____

   _____

   _____

   _____

3. Which obstacle do you think was potentially the most difficult? Why did
   Nehemiah's solution work?

   _____

   _____

   _____

4. Why did Nehemiah keep the trumpeter with him? What does this indicate about Nehemiah's leadership?

_____

_____

_____

_____

_____

_____

_____

5. Although the walls of Jerusalem had been in ruins for more than 150 years, chapter 6 of Nehemiah reports that the task of rebuilding them was completed in only fifty-two days. What made this remarkable task possible?

_____

_____

_____

_____

_____

_____

_____

_____

③ Jesus Taught His Disciples to Count the Cost

Luke 14:28–31

[28] *[Jesus said,] "Suppose one of you wants to build a tower. Won't you first sit down and estimate the cost to see if you have enough money to complete it?* [29] *For if you lay the foundation and are not able to finish it, everyone who sees it will ridicule you,* [30] *saying, 'This person began to build and wasn't able to finish.'*

[31] *"Or suppose a king is about to go to war against another king. Won't he first sit down and consider whether he is able with ten thousand men to oppose the one coming against him with twenty thousand?*

Study Questions

1. How much of what Jesus teaches in this passage is common sense, and how much is about leadership ability?

2. Compare the negative outcomes of a person who can't finish building a tower with those of a king who engages in a war he is unlikely to win. What do the differences imply about position and responsibility in leadership?

3. What part does experience play in estimating the cost of a tower or waging a war? If people don't have experience, what can or should they do to compensate?

LEADERSHIP INSIGHT AND REFLECTION

The three major components to navigation are vision, strategy, and execution. How did each of these come into play in the three passages of Scripture?

_____

_____

_____

_____

_____

_____

When it comes to vision, strategy, and execution, which is your greatest strength? Why? Which is your greatest weakness? Why?

_____

_____

_____

_____

_____

TAKING ACTION

To improve your ability to navigate for your team or organization, should you currently develop your greatest strength, or should you improve your area of weakness through growth and/or staffing? Explain what you will do and when you will start.

_____

_____

_____

_____

_____

_____

GROUP DISCUSSION QUESTIONS

1. People reading Scripture might be tempted to believe that leadership is always easy for leaders who have heard from God and have been assured that God is with them. What challenges do you think Joshua faced when attacking Ai?

2. The first attack on Ai failed because one of the Israelites disobeyed God by keeping some of the plunder when Jericho fell. If you had been in Joshua's situation after that first failure, would you have led differently? Explain.

3. Joshua was directed by God to attack Ai. However, the rebuilding of Jerusalem's walls was Nehemiah's desire, and there is no evidence in Scripture indicating that God ordered him to do it. How do you think the difference between their motivations impacted these two men's leadership? How would yours have been different?

4. What does the story from Nehemiah teach you about leadership in the midst of criticism and conflict? How might you apply it to your current situation?

5. Jesus spoke about the cost of discipleship in the Luke passage. What similarities do following Jesus and leading others have?

6. What was your greatest takeaway about navigating for other people in this lesson?

7. What change do you believe God is asking you to make in how you lead as a result of this lesson? When and how will you do it?

LESSON 5

THE LAW OF ADDITION

Leaders Add Value by Serving Others

DEFINITION OF THE LAW

Why should leaders lead? And when they do, what is their first responsibility? Many people view leadership the same way they view success, hoping to go as far as they can, to climb the ladder, to achieve the highest position possible for their talent. But contrary to conventional thinking, the bottom line in leadership isn't how far we advance ourselves but how far we advance others. That is achieved by serving others and adding value to their lives.

The interaction between every leader and follower is a relationship, and all relationships either add to or subtract from a person's life. If you are a leader, you are having either a positive or a negative impact on the people you lead. How can you tell? There is one critical question:

Are you making things better for the people who follow you?

That's it. If you cannot answer with an unhesitating yes, and give some evidence that backs it up, then you may very well be a subtractor. Most subtractors don't realize they are subtracting from others. It's unintentional. Leaders who add value to others do so intentionally. They get out of their comfort zone and choose to act unselfishly every day. Those who subtract end up dividing their impact. Those who add value to others multiply their impact.

The people who make the greatest difference seem to understand this. Many winners of the Nobel Peace Prize, like Albert Schweitzer, Martin Luther King Jr., Mother Teresa, and Bishop Desmond Tutu, were interested less in their position and more in their positive impact on others. They worked to make things better, to add value to people's lives. They didn't set out to receive a prize; they desired to engage in noble service to their fellow human beings. A servant's mindset permeated their thinking. The best place for a leader isn't always the top position. It isn't the most prominent or powerful place. It's the place where he or she can serve the best and add the most value to other people.

Leaders who add value start by valuing others. They see value that people might not even see in themselves, and they communicate that value through their words and actions. They also make themselves more valuable. They are intentional about learning and growing so that they always have something to offer their followers. They know and relate to what others value by becoming excellent listeners. They listen, learn, then lead. As a result, everybody wins—the organization, the leader, and the followers.

Most importantly, leaders who add value do the things that God values. God desires for us to not only treat people with respect but also to actively reach out to them and serve them.

That standard for conduct should influence everything a leader does, because the more power we have, the greater our impact on others—for better or worse. When you strive to lift your followers up, help them advance, make them a part of something bigger than themselves, and assist them in becoming who they were made to be, you are adding value to them. And that is the key to the Law of Addition.

CASE STUDIES

Read these case studies from the Bible and answer the study questions that follow.

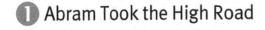 ## Abram Took the High Road

Genesis 13:1–12

¹ So Abram went up from Egypt to the Negev, with his wife and everything he had, and Lot went with him. ² Abram had become very wealthy in livestock and in silver and gold.

³ From the Negev he went from place to place until he came to Bethel, to the place between Bethel and Ai where his tent had been earlier ⁴ and where he had first built an altar. There Abram called on the name of the LORD.

⁵ Now Lot, who was moving about with Abram, also had flocks and herds and tents. ⁶ But the land could not support them while they stayed together, for their possessions were so great that they were not able to stay together. ⁷ And quarreling arose between Abram's herders and Lot's. The Canaanites and Perizzites were also living in the land at that time.

⁸ So Abram said to Lot, "Let's not have any quarreling between you and me, or between your herders and mine, for we are close relatives. ⁹ Is not the whole land before you? Let's part company. If you go to the left, I'll go to the right; if you go to the right, I'll go to the left."

¹⁰ Lot looked around and saw that the whole plain of the Jordan toward Zoar was well watered, like the garden of the LORD, like the land of Egypt. (This was before the LORD destroyed Sodom and Gomorrah.) ¹¹ So Lot chose for himself the whole plain of the Jordan and set out toward the east. The two men parted company: ¹² Abram lived in the land of Canaan, while Lot lived among the cities of the plain and pitched his tents near Sodom.

Study Questions

1. What do you think Abram's motivation was for suggesting that he and his nephew Lot go their separate ways?

_____

_____

_____

_____

_____

_____

_____

2. When Abram suggested that they separate, he did not attempt to influence what land Lot would pick, nor did Abram try to divide things evenly beforehand. He allowed Lot to do whatever he wanted. What do you think of that as a leadership strategy? Explain.

_____

_____

_____

_____

_____

3. It appears that Lot picked the more advantageous territory, since water is highly valued in that part of the world. How would you have responded to that had you been the leader? Why do you think Abram did not object?

_____

_____

_____

_____

_____

❷ Jesus Gave a New Definition of Leadership

Mark 10:35–45

35 Then James and John, the sons of Zebedee, came to him. "Teacher," they said, "we want you to do for us whatever we ask."

36 "What do you want me to do for you?" he asked.

37 They replied, "Let one of us sit at your right and the other at your left in your glory."

38 "You don't know what you are asking," Jesus said. "Can you drink the cup I drink or be baptized with the baptism I am baptized with?"

39 "We can," they answered.

Jesus said to them, "You will drink the cup I drink and be baptized with the baptism I am baptized with, 40 but to sit at my right or left is not for me to grant. These places belong to those for whom they have been prepared."

⁴¹ When the ten heard about this, they became indignant with James and John.⁴² Jesus called them together and said, "You know that those who are regarded as rulers of the Gentiles lord it over them, and their high officials exercise authority over them. ⁴³ Not so with you. Instead, whoever wants to become great among you must be your servant, ⁴⁴ and whoever wants to be first must be slave of all. ⁴⁵ For even the Son of Man did not come to be served, but to serve, and to give his life as a ransom for many."

Study Questions

1. What was the motivation of James and John when they made their request to Jesus?

2. Do you think James and John had carefully considered what Jesus was asking them before they responded, "We can," or do you think they answered quickly without thinking? Do you believe their thinking changed after Jesus said, "You will"? Explain.

3. Why do you think the other ten disciples became indignant with James and John?

4. Jesus suggested someone becomes "great" by being a servant. How is that possible?

_____

_____

_____

_____

_____

_____

③ Paul Encouraged Putting Others First

Philippians 2:1–11

¹ Therefore if you have any encouragement from being united with Christ, if any comfort from his love, if any common sharing in the Spirit, if any tenderness and compassion, ² then make my joy complete by being like-minded, having the same love, being one in spirit and of one mind. ³ Do nothing out of selfish ambition or vain conceit. Rather, in humility value others above yourselves, ⁴ not looking to your own interests but each of you to the interests of the others.
⁵ In your relationships with one another, have the same mindset as Christ Jesus:

⁶ Who, being in very nature God,
    did not consider equality with God something to be used to his own
    advantage;
⁷ rather, he made himself nothing
    by taking the very nature of a servant,
    being made in human likeness.
⁸ And being found in appearance as a man,
    he humbled himself
    by becoming obedient to death—
    even death on a cross!

⁹ Therefore God exalted him to the highest place
    and gave him the name that is above every name,

> [10] *that at the name of Jesus every knee should bow,*
>   *in heaven and on earth and under the earth,*
> [11] *and every tongue acknowledge that Jesus Christ is Lord,*
>   *to the glory of God the Father.*

Study Questions

1. Jesus had position and power as God, yet he humbled himself and made himself nothing. Why did he do that?

_____

_____

_____

_____

_____

_____

2. The passage says that Jesus took on the very nature of a servant. What differences are there between someone who serves others and someone who takes on the very nature of a servant?

_____

_____

_____

_____

_____

_____

3. Does having position and power make it harder or easier to serve others? Explain.

_____

_____

_____

_____

_____

_____

4. What are the differences between people who use leadership for their own advantage and those who use it to help and serve others?

_____

_____

_____

_____

_____

_____

_____

5. What can leaders do to prevent themselves from becoming self-serving?

_____

_____

_____

_____

_____

_____

_____

LEADERSHIP INSIGHT AND REFLECTION

In your current season and situation, how can you use whatever power and position you have to best serve others, especially the people you lead?

_____

_____

_____

_____

_____

_____

_____

_____

_____

_____

What attitudes, objectives, and actions must you change in order to become more humble and obedient, as Jesus was?

_____

_____

_____

_____

_____

_____

_____

TAKING ACTION

What specific actions will you take this week to add value to the people you lead by serving them?

_____

_____

_____

_____

_____

_____

_____

_____

_____

_____

_____

_____

_____

_____

_____

_____

_____

_____

GROUP DISCUSSION QUESTIONS

1. Instead of the way he chose, what other methods could Abram have used to handle the conflict caused by the fact that the land could not accommodate both his and Lot's herds? How would you have handled the situation? Explain.

2. In our current culture, ambition is seen as good. Why did Jesus thwart the ambition of James and John to sit on either side of him in his glory?

3. Jesus' statements that to be great one must serve and that to be first one must be the slave of all implies there may be degrees of service and reward for service. How would you interpret that idea?

4. How does emotional security or its absence in leaders impact their willingness to serve others?

5. What can leaders do to become more secure and more willing to serve?

6. What was your greatest takeaway about adding value to people in this lesson?

7. What change in your leadership do you believe God is asking you to make as a result of this lesson? When and how will you do it?

LESSON 6

THE LAW OF SOLID GROUND

Trust Is the Foundation of Leadership

DEFINITION OF THE LAW

How important is trust for a leader? It is *the most important* thing. Trust is the foundation of leadership. It is the glue that holds an organization together. Whenever you lead people, they essentially consent to take a journey with you. They will only agree to the journey if they trust the leader. And they will only continue to follow if they continue to trust. Trust makes leadership possible. That is the Law of Solid Ground.

How does a leader build trust? By demonstrating competence, connection, and, above all, character. People will forgive occasional mistakes in execution, especially if they can see that you're still growing as a leader. And they will give a leader some time to connect. But they won't trust someone who has lapses in character.

Good character is the most important factor in building trust. It communicates several things to followers:

Consistency: Leaders without character cannot be counted on day after day because their ability to perform is unreliable. If your people don't know what to expect from you as a leader, at some point they won't look to you for leadership.

Potential: Weak character is limiting. Who do you think has the greater potential to achieve great dreams and have a positive impact on others: someone who is honest, disciplined, and hardworking, or someone who is deceitful, impulsive, and lazy? Talent alone is never enough. It must be bolstered by character if a person desires to go far. In addition, when a leader's character is strong, people trust him, and they trust in his ability to release their potential. That not only gives followers hope for the future, but it also promotes a strong belief in themselves and their organization.

Respect: When you don't have character within, you can't earn respect without. Respect depends on trust. It grows when leaders make sound decisions, admit mistakes, and put what's best for their followers and the organization ahead of their personal agenda.

Trust is the foundation of leadership. Another way to describe it is as change in a leader's pocket. Each time you make good leadership decisions, you earn more change. Each time you make poor decisions, you pay out some of your change to the people. All leaders have a certain amount of change in their pocket when they start in a new leadership position. Whatever they do either builds up their change or depletes it. If leaders make one bad decision after another, they keep paying out change. Then one day, after making one last bad decision, they suddenly—and irreparably—run out of change. It doesn't even matter if the last blunder was big or small. At that point it's too late. When you're out of change, you're out as the leader. In contrast, leaders who keep making good decisions and keep recording wins for the organization build up change. Then even if they make a huge blunder, they still have plenty of change left over. When leaders abide by the Law of Solid Ground, their people trust and follow them.

CASE STUDIES

Read these case studies from the Bible and answer the study questions that follow.

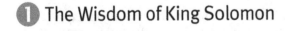 The Wisdom of King Solomon

Proverbs 16:8–18

> ⁸ *Better a little with righteousness*
> *than much gain with injustice.*
> ⁹ *In their hearts humans plan their course,*
> *but the* LORD *establishes their steps.*

¹⁰ The lips of a king speak as an oracle,
    and his mouth does not betray justice.
¹¹ Honest scales and balances belong to the LORD;
    all the weights in the bag are of his making.
¹² Kings detest wrongdoing,
    for a throne is established through righteousness.
¹³ Kings take pleasure in honest lips;
    they value the one who speaks what is right.
¹⁴ A king's wrath is a messenger of death,
    but the wise will appease it.
¹⁵ When a king's face brightens, it means life;
    his favor is like a rain cloud in spring.
¹⁶ How much better to get wisdom than gold,
    to get insight rather than silver!
¹⁷ The highway of the upright avoids evil;
    those who guard their ways preserve their lives.
¹⁸ Pride goes before destruction,
    a haughty spirit before a fall.

Study Questions

1. What are the leadership implications of the writer's statement that it's better to be poor and righteous than rich and unjust?

_____

_____

_____

_____

2. What characteristics are ascribed to kings in this passage? List as many as you find.

_____

_____

_____

_____

_____

3. Are these characteristics descriptive of kings only, of all leaders, or of what the ideal leader *should* be? Explain.

_____

_____

_____

_____

_____

_____

4. How does someone acquire these characteristics?

_____

_____

_____

_____

_____

_____

_____

❷ Character Develops from the Inside Out

Matthew 23:1–7, 25–28

[1] *Then Jesus said to the crowds and to his disciples:* [2] *"The teachers of the law and the Pharisees sit in Moses' seat.* [3] *So you must be careful to do everything they tell you. But do not do what they do, for they do not practice what they preach.* [4] *They tie up heavy, cumbersome loads and put them on other people's shoulders, but they themselves are not willing to lift a finger to move them.*

[5] *"Everything they do is done for people to see: They make their phylacteries wide and the tassels on their garments long;* [6] *they love the place of honor at banquets and the most important seats in the synagogues;* [7] *they love to be greeted with respect in the marketplaces and to be called 'Rabbi' by others. . . .*

[25] *"Woe to you, teachers of the law and Pharisees, you hypocrites! You clean the outside of the cup and dish, but inside they are full of greed and*

self-indulgence. ²⁶ Blind Pharisee! First clean the inside of the cup and dish, and then the outside also will be clean.

²⁷ "Woe to you, teachers of the law and Pharisees, you hypocrites! You are like whitewashed tombs, which look beautiful on the outside but on the inside are full of the bones of the dead and everything unclean. ²⁸ In the same way, on the outside you appear to people as righteous but on the inside you are full of hypocrisy and wickedness."

Study Questions

1. What was the motivation of the teachers of the law and Pharisees?

2. Why do you think they put difficult expectations on other people?

3. In your opinion, do you think the people trusted the teachers of the law and Pharisees before Jesus pointed out their hypocrisy? What about afterward? Explain.

4. Jesus made it clear the people were not to follow the example of these hypocritical leaders, but why did he tell people to obey them?

_____

_____

_____

_____

_____

5. When people have leaders who "don't practice what they preach," what happens to the people? What happens to the leaders? What happens to the team or organization? How effective are their results?

_____

_____

_____

_____

_____

_____

_____

_____

_____

❸ Peter Gives Instruction

1 Peter 5:1–11

¹ To the elders among you, I appeal as a fellow elder and a witness of Christ's sufferings who also will share in the glory to be revealed: ² Be shepherds of God's flock that is under your care, watching over them—not because you must, but because you are willing, as God wants you to be; not pursuing dishonest gain, but eager to serve; ³ not lording it over those entrusted to you, but being examples to the flock. ⁴ And when the Chief Shepherd appears, you will receive the crown of glory that will never fade away.

⁵ In the same way, you who are younger, submit yourselves to your elders. All of you, clothe yourselves with humility toward one another, because,

> "God opposes the proud
>   but shows favor to the humble."

⁶ Humble yourselves, therefore, under God's mighty hand, that he may lift you up in due time. ⁷ Cast all your anxiety on him because he cares for you.

⁸ Be alert and of sober mind. Your enemy the devil prowls around like a roaring lion looking for someone to devour. ⁹ Resist him, standing firm in the faith, because you know that the family of believers throughout the world is undergoing the same kind of sufferings.

¹⁰ And the God of all grace, who called you to his eternal glory in Christ, after you have suffered a little while, will himself restore you and make you strong, firm and steadfast. ¹¹ To him be the power for ever and ever. Amen.

Study Questions

1. Peter starts by saying that he is an elder who is speaking to fellow elders. Why does he do that?

   _____

   _____

   _____

   _____

2. What characteristics and actions does Peter suggest leaders should possess? How should they develop trust?

   _____

   _____

   _____

   _____

3. Why does Peter tell leaders to cast their anxiety on God? What kinds of things do leaders do when they are anxious?

   _____

   _____

   _____

   _____

4. Paul directs leaders to be humble under God's mighty hand so that they may be lifted up at some later time. How should this impact leaders' attitudes and approach to leading others?

_____

_____

_____

_____

_____

_____

LEADERSHIP INSIGHT AND REFLECTION

All three passages in this lesson contain leadership advice from an experienced leader to other leaders. What do all the passages have in common?

_____

_____

_____

_____

_____

_____

_____

Which instruction or advice about leadership struck a chord within you? What have you recently done or are you currently doing that is undermining trust with the people you lead rather than strengthening it?

_____

_____

_____

_____

_____

_____

_____

TAKING ACTION

What specific action will you take this week to correct where you are undermining trust? Do you need to apologize to someone? Do you need to make something right? Do you need to confess a habitual sin to an accountability partner? Do you need to break a habit?

_____
_____
_____
_____
_____
_____
_____

What will you do?

_____
_____
_____
_____
_____
_____
_____
_____
_____
_____
_____

When will you do it?   Date: _____

GROUP DISCUSSION QUESTIONS

1. Have you ever worked with a leader you could not trust? What did the leader do? How did it impact you? What was the ultimate result for you and the team?

2. Does the importance of developing trust change, becoming more or less important, when someone has a formal leadership position, such as king, teacher, elder, or appointed leader? Explain your answer.

3. What is the fastest way to build trust with people you follow?

4. Are your faith and obedience to Christ connected to your leadership role with others? If so, how? If not, should they be?

5. Which of the three passages did you most relate to and why?

6. Is there any place in your life where you are not practicing what you preach? If so, why do you struggle in this area? How is it negatively impacting you?

7. What action or change does God desire from you as a result of what you've learned from this lesson? When and how will you do it?

THE LAW OF RESPECT

People Naturally Follow Leaders
Stronger than Themselves

DEFINITION OF THE LAW

There are only a few situations in which people willingly follow a leader they consider weaker than themselves. Perhaps they respect that leader's reputation or past accomplishments. Or they might have respect for the chain of command. But even in those cases, their willingness to follow won't last forever. Eventually they will follow unwillingly—or stop following all together. That's because people naturally follow leaders stronger than themselves. That's the Law of Respect.

We *want* to follow leaders we respect. People who score an 8 (out of 10) in leadership don't go looking for a 6 to follow—they naturally follow someone who would score a 9 or a 10. The less skilled tend to follow the more highly skilled and gifted.

Watch what happens when people get together in a group for the first time. At first, group members make tentative moves in different directions. But as they continue interacting, the voices of those with more leadership skills begin to stand out. And the others begin to instinctively respect their opinions. Before long, everyone is listening to and following the strongest leader or leaders in the group.

What makes those strong leaders stand out to everyone else? What causes one person to respect and follow another? I believe the following factors come into play:

Natural leadership ability: Let's face it; some are just born with greater ability in this area than others. All leaders are not created equal. Some just naturally stand out. But talent alone isn't enough.

Respect for others: Some would-be leaders try to dictate to the group. But they're not the ones the others turn to. Leaders that people want to follow start by showing everyone respect.

Courage: We tend to follow the person in the group who stands for something. When someone speaks with courage and conviction, they gain the respect of the group. And when they lead the charge, others follow.

Success: It's hard to argue with a good track record. When someone demonstrates success or expertise in an area, others tend to turn to them. We believe in their ability to do it again, and we follow because we want to be part of their future success.

Loyalty: In an era of free agency, change, and frequent transition, dedication is an asset. People tend to follow someone who has shown that they stick with a job until it's done, even when the going gets rough.

If others demonstrate a reluctance to follow you, it may be that their leadership level is higher than yours. That creates a difficult situation. If you're a 7 as a leader, those who are 8s, 9s, and 10s aren't likely to follow you—no matter how compelling your vision or plan. It's because of the Law of Respect. Like it or not, that's just the way leadership works.

So what can you do about it? Become a better leader. There's always hope for a leader who wants to grow. People who are naturally a 7 may never become a 10—but they can become a 9. There is always room to grow. And the more you grow, the better the people you will attract. Why? Because people naturally follow leaders stronger than themselves.

CASE STUDIES

Read these case studies from the Bible and answer the study questions that follow.

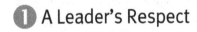 **A Leader's Respect**

Judges 4:1–16

> [1] *Again the Israelites did evil in the eyes of the Lord, now that Ehud was dead.*
> [2] *So the Lord sold them into the hands of Jabin king of Canaan, who reigned*

in Hazor. Sisera, the commander of his army, was based in Harosheth Haggoyim. ³ Because he had nine hundred chariots fitted with iron and had cruelly oppressed the Israelites for twenty years, they cried to the LORD for help.

⁴ Now Deborah, a prophet, the wife of Lappidoth, was leading Israel at that time. ⁵ She held court under the Palm of Deborah between Ramah and Bethel in the hill country of Ephraim, and the Israelites went up to her to have their disputes decided. ⁶ She sent for Barak son of Abinoam from Kedesh in Naphtali and said to him, "The LORD, the God of Israel, commands you: 'Go, take with you ten thousand men of Naphtali and Zebulun and lead them up to Mount Tabor. ⁷ I will lead Sisera, the commander of Jabin's army, with his chariots and his troops to the Kishon River and give him into your hands.'"

⁸ Barak said to her, "If you go with me, I will go; but if you don't go with me, I won't go."

⁹ "Certainly I will go with you," said Deborah. "But because of the course you are taking, the honor will not be yours, for the LORD will deliver Sisera into the hands of a woman." So Deborah went with Barak to Kedesh. ¹⁰ There Barak summoned Zebulun and Naphtali, and ten thousand men went up under his command. Deborah also went up with him.

¹¹ Now Heber the Kenite had left the other Kenites, the descendants of Hobab, Moses' brother-in-law, and pitched his tent by the great tree in Zaanannim near Kedesh.

¹² When they told Sisera that Barak son of Abinoam had gone up to Mount Tabor, ¹³ Sisera summoned from Harosheth Haggoyim to the Kishon River all his men and his nine hundred chariots fitted with iron.

¹⁴ Then Deborah said to Barak, "Go! This is the day the LORD has given Sisera into your hands. Has not the LORD gone ahead of you?" So Barak went down Mount Tabor, with ten thousand men following him. ¹⁵ At Barak's advance, the LORD routed Sisera and all his chariots and army by the sword, and Sisera got down from his chariot and fled on foot.

¹⁶ Barak pursued the chariots and army as far as Harosheth Haggoyim, and all Sisera's troops fell by the sword; not a man was left.

Study Questions

1. Why do you believe Barak was unwilling to go to battle without Deborah?

   _____

   _____

   _____

   _____

2. How unusual do you think it was at that time for a woman to be leading a nation of people like the Israelites? What does that say about Deborah's level of leadership?

   _____

   _____

   _____

   _____

   _____

3. God should be credited for the victory because he told the Israelites that he was giving the Canaanites into their hands to be defeated. But which leader had a greater role in fulfilling what God wanted done: Deborah or Barak? Explain.

   _____

   _____

   _____

   _____

   _____

② The Prince's Loyalty

1 Samuel 20:1–13, 16–17, 24–31

¹ Then David fled from Naioth at Ramah and went to Jonathan and asked, "What have I done? What is my crime? How have I wronged your father, that he is trying to kill me?"

² "Never!" Jonathan replied. "You are not going to die! Look, my father doesn't do anything, great or small, without letting me know. Why would he hide this from me? It isn't so!"

³ But David took an oath and said, "Your father knows very well that I have found favor in your eyes, and he has said to himself, 'Jonathan must not know this or he will be grieved.' Yet as surely as the LORD lives and as you live, there is only a step between me and death."

⁴ Jonathan said to David, "Whatever you want me to do, I'll do for you."

⁵ So David said, "Look, tomorrow is the New Moon feast, and I am supposed to dine with the king; but let me go and hide in the field until the evening of the day after tomorrow. ⁶ If your father misses me at all, tell him, 'David earnestly asked my permission to hurry to Bethlehem, his hometown, because an annual sacrifice is being made there for his whole clan.' ⁷ If he says, 'Very well,' then your servant is safe. But if he loses his temper, you can be sure that he is determined to harm me. ⁸ As for you, show kindness to your servant, for you have brought him into a covenant with you before the LORD. If I am guilty, then kill me yourself! Why hand me over to your father?"

⁹ "Never!" Jonathan said. "If I had the least inkling that my father was determined to harm you, wouldn't I tell you?"

¹⁰ David asked, "Who will tell me if your father answers you harshly?"

¹¹ "Come," Jonathan said, "let's go out into the field." So they went there together.

¹² Then Jonathan said to David, "I swear by the LORD, the God of Israel, that I will surely sound out my father by this time the day after tomorrow! If he is favorably disposed toward you, will I not send you word and let you know? ¹³ But if my father intends to harm you, may the LORD deal with Jonathan, be it ever so severely, if I do not let you know and send you away in peace. May the LORD be with you as he has been with my father. . . .

¹⁶ So Jonathan made a covenant with the house of David, saying, "May the LORD call David's enemies to account." ¹⁷ And Jonathan had David reaffirm his oath out of love for him, because he loved him as he loved himself. . . .

²⁴ So David hid in the field, and when the New Moon feast came, the king sat down to eat. ²⁵ He sat in his customary place by the wall, opposite Jonathan, and Abner sat next to Saul, but David's place was empty. ²⁶ Saul said nothing that day, for he thought, "Something must have happened to David to make him ceremonially unclean—surely he is unclean." ²⁷ But the next day, the second day

of the month, David's place was empty again. Then Saul said to his son Jonathan, "Why hasn't the son of Jesse come to the meal, either yesterday or today?"

²⁸ Jonathan answered, "David earnestly asked me for permission to go to Bethlehem. ²⁹ He said, 'Let me go, because our family is observing a sacrifice in the town and my brother has ordered me to be there. If I have found favor in your eyes, let me get away to see my brothers.' That is why he has not come to the king's table."

³⁰ Saul's anger flared up at Jonathan and he said to him, "You son of a perverse and rebellious woman! Don't I know that you have sided with the son of Jesse to your own shame and to the shame of the mother who bore you? ³¹ As long as the son of Jesse lives on this earth, neither you nor your kingdom will be established. Now send someone to bring him to me, for he must die!"

Study Questions

1. What does Jonathan's loyalty communicate about David's leadership?

_____

_____

_____

2. What does Saul's anger and hostility say about David's leadership? What does it say about Saul?

_____

_____

_____

3. What do you think would have ultimately happened to David, Jonathan, and Saul if Jonathan had sided with his father instead of David?

_____

_____

_____

_____

_____

③ The Writing on the Wall

Daniel 5:1–12, 17, 22–30

[1] *King Belshazzar gave a great banquet for a thousand of his nobles and drank wine with them.* [2] *While Belshazzar was drinking his wine, he gave orders to bring in the gold and silver goblets that Nebuchadnezzar his father had taken from the temple in Jerusalem, so that the king and his nobles, his wives and his concubines might drink from them.* [3] *So they brought in the gold goblets that had been taken from the temple of God in Jerusalem, and the king and his nobles, his wives and his concubines drank from them.*
[4] *As they drank the wine, they praised the gods of gold and silver, of bronze, iron, wood and stone.*

[5] *Suddenly the fingers of a human hand appeared and wrote on the plaster of the wall, near the lampstand in the royal palace. The king watched the hand as it wrote.* [6] *His face turned pale and he was so frightened that his legs became weak and his knees were knocking.*

[7] *The king summoned the enchanters, astrologers and diviners. Then he said to these wise men of Babylon, "Whoever reads this writing and tells me what it means will be clothed in purple and have a gold chain placed around his neck, and he will be made the third highest ruler in the kingdom."*

[8] *Then all the king's wise men came in, but they could not read the writing or tell the king what it meant.* [9] *So King Belshazzar became even more terrified and his face grew more pale. His nobles were baffled.*

[10] *The queen, hearing the voices of the king and his nobles, came into the banquet hall. "May the king live forever!" she said. "Don't be alarmed! Don't look so pale!* [11] *There is a man in your kingdom who has the spirit of the holy gods in him. In the time of your father he was found to have insight and intelligence and wisdom like that of the gods. Your father, King Nebuchadnezzar, appointed him chief of the magicians, enchanters, astrologers and diviners.* [12] *He did this because Daniel, whom the king called Belteshazzar, was found to have a keen mind and knowledge and understanding, and also the ability to interpret dreams, explain riddles and solve difficult problems. Call for Daniel, and he will tell you what the writing means.". . .*

¹⁷ Then Daniel answered the king, "You may keep your gifts for yourself and give your rewards to someone else. Nevertheless, I will read the writing for the king and tell him what it means. . . .

²² "But you, Belshazzar . . . have not humbled yourself. . . . ²³ Instead, you have set yourself up against the Lord of heaven. . . . You did not honor the God who holds in his hand your life and all your ways. ²⁴ Therefore he sent the hand that wrote the inscription. . . .

²⁵ "This is the inscription that was written:

MENE, MENE, TEKEL, PARSIN

²⁶ "Here is what these words mean:

Mene: God has numbered the days of your reign and brought it to an end.
²⁷ Tekel: You have been weighed on the scales and found wanting.
²⁸ Peres: Your kingdom is divided and given to the Medes and Persians."

²⁹ Then at Belshazzar's command, Daniel was clothed in purple, a gold chain was placed around his neck, and he was proclaimed the third highest ruler in the kingdom.

³⁰ That very night Belshazzar, king of the Babylonians, was slain, ³¹ and Darius the Mede took over the kingdom, at the age of sixty-two.

Study Questions

1. Even though Daniel was an exile from Judah and a slave, he rose to become ruler over the province of Babylon, a high official under Nebuchadnezzar. Why do you think the queen remembered Daniel while King Belshazzar did not?

_____

_____

_____

_____

_____

2. If leadership is influence, was Daniel a leader before King Belshazzar sought him out? What about afterward?

_____

_____

_____

_____

_____

_____

3. King Belshazzar promised to honor whoever could read and interpret the writing. When Daniel did that, he gave the king terrible news, yet the king honored the promise he made. Why?

_____

_____

_____

_____

_____

_____

LEADERSHIP INSIGHT AND REFLECTION

Think about the leaders mentioned in this lesson's passages:

- Deborah
- Barak
- Jabin, king of Canaan
- Sisera, the commander of Jabin's army
- Jonathan
- David
- Saul, king of Israel
- Belshazzar, king of Babylon
- The queen of Babylon
- Daniel

Which leader do you respect the most? Why? Which do you respect least? Why?

_____
_____
_____
_____
_____
_____
_____

Which best describes you?

- A leader that team members respect and follow
- A leader that team members don't follow
- A team member who follows a respected leader
- A team member who must follow an unrespected leader

Explain your answer.

_____
_____
_____
_____
_____
_____
_____

If you answered anything other than the first response to the previous question and you desire to be a leader that others respect and follow, what do you lack to get there? Your answer may require you to make difficult changes in character, skills, habits, or situation.

_____
_____
_____
_____
_____
_____

TAKING ACTION

Think about your answer to the last question: what you currently lack to become a respected leader. Keeping in mind that the leader makes the position, and the position does not make the leader, write a plan for how you can become the kind of leader others will respect and follow.

_____

_____

_____

_____

_____

_____

_____

_____

_____

_____

_____

_____

_____

_____

_____

_____

_____

_____

_____

_____

_____

The date you will take the first step of your plan: _____

The date by which you desire to reach your goal: _____

GROUP DISCUSSION QUESTIONS

1. For what purpose did Deborah tell Barak that the honor would not be his but would go to a woman? What do you believe was her motive?

2. Did Barak make the right or wrong decision in asking Deborah to go with him? Why?

3. Saul and Belshazzar were both kings who found out their reigns were about to end because they treated God without the reverence he deserves. How did each of them respond to that knowledge?

4. After the prophet Samuel told Saul that God had rejected him as king (1 Samuel 15:24), Saul sensed that David was going to overtake him as leader. How do you respond to a leader who is advancing ahead of you?

5. Daniel was the deliverer of the worst kind of news to Belshazzar. How do you think Daniel felt having to do it? How do you respond in those kinds of situations? Do they strike you as conversations to fear or opportunities to influence? Explain.

6. What was your greatest takeaway from this lesson about the dynamics of influence and how weaker leaders follow stronger ones?

7. What changes in your leadership do you believe God is asking you to make as a result of this lesson? How do you intend to change and when will you take action?

LESSON 8

THE LAW OF INTUITION

Leaders Evaluate Everything with a Leadership Bias

DEFINITION OF THE LAW

Every person is intuitive in some way in an area where they are naturally talented or experienced, whether it's football, or public speaking, or engineering. Top performers in a field evaluate every situation with a bias based on their expertise. Good leaders are no different. They evaluate everything with a leadership bias. And while naturally talented leaders may start with more intuition in this area, everyone who wants to lead can increase their leadership intuition.

Intuition is not concrete. It doesn't rely on empirical evidence alone. Instead, it is an instinct informed by talent, knowledge, and experience. It's like a lens through which we see the facts based on who we are and what we already know. This is valuable because it enables us to rapidly predict problems, make decisions, and seize opportunities. It often helps us avoid being surprised or blindsided.

Leadership intuition is based on measurable data plus instinct about intangible factors, such as employee morale, organizational momentum, or relational dynamics. Good leaders instinctively, almost automatically, know how to lead in any situation. For them, leadership issues just jump out. And they are able to react more quickly than less skilled leaders can.

Effective leaders are readers of situations, trends, opportunities, and people. They have a habit of examining these things through a leadership lens. Even if you don't already have that instinct or habit, you can develop it.

Read situations like a leader by looking at the small details. Pay attention to progress and try to assess whether things are humming along or about to grind to a halt. Read trends like a leader by looking ahead. Expand your view and take in the big picture. Use what's happening now to predict where things are headed. Read people like a leader by looking deeper than the surface. Ask questions and listen. And try to discover motives and attitudes.

You can develop leadership intuition in the same way that a person becomes intuitive in any area: by supplementing natural talent with as much knowledge and experience as possible. Make a commitment to learn and grow as a leader. Strive daily to evaluate everything with a leadership bias. As you apply experience and use your instincts, you will reap the benefits of the Law of Intuition.

CASE STUDIES

Read these case studies from the Bible and answer the study questions that follow.

❶ A Leader with Intuition Saves Lives

1 Samuel 25:2–35, 38–39

[2] A certain man in Maon, who had property there at Carmel, was very wealthy. He had a thousand goats and three thousand sheep, which he was shearing in Carmel. [3] His name was Nabal and his wife's name was Abigail. She was an intelligent and beautiful woman, but her husband was surly and mean in his dealings—he was a Calebite.

[4] While David was in the wilderness, he heard that Nabal was shearing sheep. [5] So he sent ten young men and said to them, "Go up to Nabal at Carmel and greet him in my name. [6] Say to him: 'Long life to you! Good health to you and your household! And good health to all that is yours!

7 "'Now I hear that it is sheep-shearing time. When your shepherds were with us, we did not mistreat them, and the whole time they were at Carmel nothing of theirs was missing. 8 Ask your own servants and they will tell you. Therefore be favorable toward my men, since we come at a festive time. Please give your servants and your son David whatever you can find for them.'"

9 When David's men arrived, they gave Nabal this message in David's name. Then they waited.

10 Nabal answered David's servants, "Who is this David? Who is this son of Jesse? Many servants are breaking away from their masters these days. 11 Why should I take my bread and water, and the meat I have slaughtered for my shearers, and give it to men coming from who knows where?"

12 David's men turned around and went back. When they arrived, they reported every word. 13 David said to his men, "Each of you strap on your sword!" So they did, and David strapped his on as well. About four hundred men went up with David, while two hundred stayed with the supplies.

14 One of the servants told Abigail, Nabal's wife, "David sent messengers from the wilderness to give our master his greetings, but he hurled insults at them. 15 Yet these men were very good to us. They did not mistreat us, and the whole time we were out in the fields near them nothing was missing. 16 Night and day they were a wall around us the whole time we were herding our sheep near them. 17 Now think it over and see what you can do, because disaster is hanging over our master and his whole household. He is such a wicked man that no one can talk to him."

18 Abigail acted quickly. She took two hundred loaves of bread, two skins of wine, five dressed sheep, five seahs of roasted grain, a hundred cakes of raisins and two hundred cakes of pressed figs, and loaded them on donkeys. 19 Then she told her servants, "Go on ahead; I'll follow you." But she did not tell her husband Nabal.

20 As she came riding her donkey into a mountain ravine, there were David and his men descending toward her, and she met them. 21 David had just said, "It's been useless—all my watching over this fellow's property in the wilderness so that nothing of his was missing. He has paid me back evil for good. 22 May God deal with David, be it ever so severely, if by morning I leave alive one male of all who belong to him!"

²³ When Abigail saw David, she quickly got off her donkey and bowed down before David with her face to the ground. ²⁴ She fell at his feet and said: "Pardon your servant, my lord, and let me speak to you; hear what your servant has to say. ²⁵ Please pay no attention, my lord, to that wicked man Nabal. He is just like his name—his name means Fool, and folly goes with him. And as for me, your servant, I did not see the men my lord sent. ²⁶ And now, my lord, as surely as the LORD your God lives and as you live, since the LORD has kept you from bloodshed and from avenging yourself with your own hands, may your enemies and all who are intent on harming my lord be like Nabal. ²⁷ And let this gift, which your servant has brought to my lord, be given to the men who follow you.

²⁸ "Please forgive your servant's presumption. The LORD your God will certainly make a lasting dynasty for my lord, because you fight the LORD's battles, and no wrongdoing will be found in you as long as you live. ²⁹ Even though someone is pursuing you to take your life, the life of my lord will be bound securely in the bundle of the living by the LORD your God, but the lives of your enemies he will hurl away as from the pocket of a sling. ³⁰ When the LORD has fulfilled for my lord every good thing he promised concerning him and has appointed him ruler over Israel, ³¹ my lord will not have on his conscience the staggering burden of needless bloodshed or of having avenged himself. And when the LORD your God has brought my lord success, remember your servant."

³² David said to Abigail, "Praise be to the LORD, the God of Israel, who has sent you today to meet me. ³³ May you be blessed for your good judgment and for keeping me from bloodshed this day and from avenging myself with my own hands. ³⁴ Otherwise, as surely as the LORD, the God of Israel, lives, who has kept me from harming you, if you had not come quickly to meet me, not one male belonging to Nabal would have been left alive by daybreak."

³⁵ Then David accepted from her hand what she had brought him and said, "Go home in peace. I have heard your words and granted your request." . . .

³⁸ About ten days later, the LORD struck Nabal and he died.

³⁹ When David heard that Nabal was dead, he . . . sent word to Abigail, asking her to become his wife.

Study Questions

1. How did the servant who talked to Abigail exhibit intuition?

   _____

   _____

   _____

   _____

2. Taking into account all that Abigail did, said, and told her servants to do, how many leadership insights did she display?

   _____

   _____

   _____

   _____

   _____

3. What would have happened if Abigail had not taken action? Play out the story and imagine what would have happened to Nabal, his household, Abigail, and David. Include any changes that might have occurred to David's later reign as king.

   _____

   _____

   _____

   _____

   _____

   _____

② The Wisdom of Solomon

1 Kings 3:16–28

16 Now two prostitutes came to the king and stood before him. 17 One of them said, "Pardon me, my lord. This woman and I live in the same house, and I had a baby while she was there with me. *18* The third day after my child was born, this woman also had a baby. We were alone; there was no one in the house but the two of us.

19 "During the night this woman's son died because she lay on him. *20* So she got up in the middle of the night and took my son from my side while I your servant was asleep. She put him by her breast and put her dead son by my breast. *21* The next morning, I got up to nurse my son—and he was dead! But when I looked at him closely in the morning light, I saw that it wasn't the son I had borne."

22 The other woman said, "No! The living one is my son; the dead one is yours."

But the first one insisted, "No! The dead one is yours; the living one is mine." And so they argued before the king.

23 The king said, "This one says, 'My son is alive and your son is dead,' while that one says, 'No! Your son is dead and mine is alive.'"

24 Then the king said, "Bring me a sword." So they brought a sword for the king. *25* He then gave an order: "Cut the living child in two and give half to one and half to the other."

26 The woman whose son was alive was deeply moved out of love for her son and said to the king, "Please, my lord, give her the living baby! Don't kill him!"

But the other said, "Neither I nor you shall have him. Cut him in two!"

27 Then the king gave his ruling: "Give the living baby to the first woman. Do not kill him; she is his mother."

28 When all Israel heard the verdict the king had given, they held the king in awe, because they saw that he had wisdom from God to administer justice.

Study Questions

1. It isn't clear from the wording in the story which woman was the mother of the living child: the woman complaining that the children had been switched or the woman who denied that it happened. As you read, which did you think was the mother of the living son? Why?

_____

_____

_____

_____

2. Do you think King Solomon knew who was telling the truth from the beginning and threatened to use the sword to prove it? Or do you think he had the wisdom to make the threat but didn't know which was which until the women spoke?

_____

_____

_____

_____

_____

3. Are you more likely to take action based on your intuition alone? Or do you usually wait until you have some kind of evidence verifying your intuition before taking action? Which is the wiser course of action?

_____

_____

_____

_____

_____

_____

❸ Barnabas Sees Paul's Potential

Acts 9:19–30

19 Saul spent several days with the disciples in Damascus. 20 At once he began to preach in the synagogues that Jesus is the Son of God. 21 All those who heard him were astonished and asked, "Isn't he the man who raised havoc in Jerusalem among those who call on this name? And hasn't he come here to take them as prisoners to the chief priests?" 22 Yet Saul grew more and more powerful and baffled the Jews living in Damascus by proving that Jesus is the Messiah.

23 After many days had gone by, there was a conspiracy among the Jews to kill him, 24 but Saul learned of their plan. Day and night they kept close watch on the city gates in order to kill him. 25 But his followers took him by night and lowered him in a basket through an opening in the wall.

²⁶ When he came to Jerusalem, he tried to join the disciples, but they were all afraid of him, not believing that he really was a disciple. ²⁷ But Barnabas took him and brought him to the apostles. He told them how Saul on his journey had seen the Lord and that the Lord had spoken to him, and how in Damascus he had preached fearlessly in the name of Jesus. ²⁸ So Saul stayed with them and moved about freely in Jerusalem, speaking boldly in the name of the Lord. ²⁹ He talked and debated with the Hellenistic Jews, but they tried to kill him. ³⁰ When the believers learned of this, they took him down to Caesarea and sent him off to Tarsus.

Study Questions

1. The Jews in Damascus were baffled by Paul's leadership and intellect. What does that say about their leadership intuition?

   _____

   _____

   _____

   _____

   _____

2. Paul had a negative reputation because of the way he persecuted the church before his conversion. How do you think Barnabas was able to see Paul's leadership potential in the face of that?

   _____

   _____

   _____

   _____

3. What does the Jerusalem disciples' initial reaction to Paul indicate about how fear impacts leadership intuition?

   _____

   _____

   _____

   _____

LEADERSHIP INSIGHT AND REFLECTION

What roles do you think wisdom, discernment, people skills, and leadership experience play in leadership intuition based on the three passages?

_____

_____

_____

_____

Rate yourself on a scale of 1 (low) to 10 (high) in each of the following areas, and briefly describe why you rated yourself that way.

Wisdom: _____

Discernment: _____

Leadership Experience: _____

People Skills/EQ: _____

Natural Leadership Intuition: _____

In which of the first four areas would you like to grow to increase your overall leadership intuition? How would growth in that area help you?

_____

_____

_____

_____

TAKING ACTION

Whatever natural leadership intuition you have is God-given. But you can improve your skills through effort and thereby increase your intuition. How will you grow in your chosen area? Be as specific as possible and give yourself a timetable for it.

_____

_____

_____

_____

GROUP DISCUSSION QUESTIONS

1. In the first passage, who possessed the greatest leadership intuition and wisdom: the unnamed servant, Abigail, or David? Explain your answer.

2. If you had been in King Solomon's shoes, what might you have done to learn the truth and deliver justice?

3. What risks was Barnabas taking when vouching for Paul and bringing him before the apostles? How do you imagine that interaction occurring? What was done and said?

4. Are you naturally intuitive or do you ordinarily base your decision-making on evidence and data? How has your natural wiring been beneficial? How does it hold you back?

5. What are the rewards of leadership intuition?

6. What was your greatest takeaway about leadership intuition from this lesson?

7. What actions do you believe God is asking you to take to further develop your leadership intuition? When and how will you do it?

THE LAW OF MAGNETISM

Who You Are Is Who You Attract

DEFINITION OF THE LAW

Effective leaders are always on the lookout for good people. In fact, even when they're not actively hiring, most leaders still carry around a mental list of the skills, personality traits, character qualities, and attitudes that they'd like future new hires to possess. You probably have a list of some kind. Think about who you would want on your team. What is your profile of the perfect employee?

Once you know who you want, how do you go about finding that kind of person? How do you attract good job candidates who possess the qualities you desire? What one thing will determine—more than anything else—whether the people you want are the people you attract? You may be surprised by the answer. Believe it or not, who you attract is not determined by what you want. It's determined by who you are.

The implications of this truth are pretty clear. If you want team members with grit, then you need to demonstrate perseverance yourself. You may wish you had team members who would plan ahead. But if you yourself tend to act quickly and sort out the results later, you'll have a hard time attracting—or keeping—those who think through their decisions. If you want useful traits in your followers, focus on developing them in yourself. Here are some characteristics that you probably consider important in a team member:

Positive attitude: Rarely have I seen positive people attracted to a negative work environment. People who view life as a series of opportunities and exciting challenges don't want to work for leaders who talk about how bad things are all the time. The good news is that attitude is a choice. When you choose to focus on the good or the growth potential in every situation, you will create a culture that positive people want to be part of.

Trustworthiness: This one is more subtle. Most of us don't consider ourselves untrustworthy. But there is more to trustworthiness than just not lying. To be worthy of trust involves telling the whole truth, keeping commitments, and acknowledging reality. If you want to attract followers who are trustworthy, be real. Only make commitments that you will keep. And don't ignore or deny troublesome issues.

Work ethic: Want team members who are willing to work hard? Then let people see you hard at work. Don't expect punctuality or a commitment to excellence from others if you come in late or do your job halfheartedly. Hard workers look for an environment where everyone is pulling their weight—especially the leader.

Your list probably includes other traits, such as perseverance, energy, or growth potential. The Law of Magnetism still applies. Who you are is who you attract. If you focus on developing the qualities in yourself that you want from others, you will build a unified team that can achieve a great deal together.

CASE STUDIES

Read these case studies from the Bible and answer the study questions that follow.

① Joshua Succeeds Moses

Exodus 17:8–14

[8] *The Amalekites came and attacked the Israelites at Rephidim.* [9] *Moses said to Joshua, "Choose some of our men and go out to fight the Amalekites. Tomorrow I will stand on top of the hill with the staff of God in my hands."*

¹⁰ So Joshua fought the Amalekites as Moses had ordered, and Moses, Aaron and Hur went to the top of the hill. ¹¹ As long as Moses held up his hands, the Israelites were winning, but whenever he lowered his hands, the Amalekites were winning. ¹² When Moses' hands grew tired, they took a stone and put it under him and he sat on it. Aaron and Hur held his hands up—one on one side, one on the other—so that his hands remained steady till sunset. ¹³ So Joshua overcame the Amalekite army with the sword.

¹⁴ Then the Lord said to Moses, "Write this on a scroll as something to be remembered and make sure that Joshua hears it, because I will completely blot out the name of Amalek from under heaven."

Exodus 33:10–11

¹⁰ Whenever the people saw the pillar of cloud standing at the entrance to the tent, they all stood and worshiped, each at the entrance to their tent. ¹¹ The Lord would speak to Moses face to face, as one speaks to a friend. Then Moses would return to the camp, but his young aide Joshua son of Nun did not leave the tent.

Numbers 27:12–13, 15–23

¹² Then the Lord said to Moses, "Go up this mountain in the Abarim Range and see the land I have given the Israelites. ¹³ After you have seen it, you too will be gathered to your people, as your brother Aaron was . . . .

¹⁵ Moses said to the Lord, ¹⁶ "May the Lord, the God who gives breath to all living things, appoint someone over this community ¹⁷ to go out and come in before them, one who will lead them out and bring them in, so the Lord's people will not be like sheep without a shepherd."

¹⁸ So the Lord said to Moses, "Take Joshua son of Nun, a man in whom is the spirit of leadership, and lay your hand on him. ¹⁹ Have him stand before Eleazar the priest and the entire assembly and commission him in their presence. ²⁰ Give him some of your authority so the whole Israelite community will obey him. ²¹ He is to stand before Eleazar the priest, who will obtain decisions for him by inquiring of the Urim before the Lord. At his command he and the entire community of the Israelites will go out, and at his command they will come in."

²² Moses did as the LORD commanded him. He took Joshua and had him stand before Eleazar the priest and the whole assembly. ²³ Then he laid his hands on him and commissioned him, as the LORD instructed through Moses.

Study Questions

1. In what ways were Moses and Joshua alike?

_____

_____

_____

_____

_____

_____

2. Joshua was one of the twelve spies Moses sent into the Promised Land to explore it and report back about it (Numbers 13). Ten of those spies were afraid and rebelled against God's plan. Joshua and Caleb were the only ones who wanted to go and conquer Canaan. How do you think this qualified Joshua to succeed Moses? What other qualifications did Joshua have?

_____

_____

_____

_____

_____

_____

❷ David's Mighty Men

1 Chronicles 11:10–25

¹⁰ These were the chiefs of David's mighty warriors—they, together with all Israel, gave his kingship strong support to extend it over the whole land, as the LORD had promised— ¹¹ this is the list of David's mighty warriors:

Jashobeam, a Hakmonite, was chief of the officers; he raised his spear against three hundred men, whom he killed in one encounter.

[12] Next to him was Eleazar son of Dodai the Ahohite, one of the three mighty warriors. [13] He was with David at Pas Dammim when the Philistines gathered there for battle. At a place where there was a field full of barley, the troops fled from the Philistines. [14] But they took their stand in the middle of the field. They defended it and struck the Philistines down, and the LORD brought about a great victory.

[15] Three of the thirty chiefs came down to David to the rock at the cave of Adullam, while a band of Philistines was encamped in the Valley of Rephaim. [16] At that time David was in the stronghold, and the Philistine garrison was at Bethlehem. [17] David longed for water and said, "Oh, that someone would get me a drink of water from the well near the gate of Bethlehem!" [18] So the Three broke through the Philistine lines, drew water from the well near the gate of Bethlehem and carried it back to David. But he refused to drink it; instead, he poured it out to the LORD. [19] "God forbid that I should do this!" he said. "Should I drink the blood of these men who went at the risk of their lives?" Because they risked their lives to bring it back, David would not drink it.

Such were the exploits of the three mighty warriors.

[20] Abishai the brother of Joab was chief of the Three. He raised his spear against three hundred men, whom he killed, and so he became as famous as the Three. [21] He was doubly honored above the Three and became their commander, even though he was not included among them.

[22] Benaiah son of Jehoiada, a valiant fighter from Kabzeel, performed great exploits. He struck down Moab's two mightiest warriors. He also went down into a pit on a snowy day and killed a lion. [23] And he struck down an Egyptian who was five cubits tall. Although the Egyptian had a spear like a weaver's rod in his hand, Benaiah went against him with a club. He snatched the spear from the Egyptian's hand and killed him with his own spear. [24] Such were the exploits of Benaiah son of Jehoiada; he too was as famous as the three mighty warriors. [25] He was held in greater honor than any of the Thirty, but he was not included among the Three. And David put him in charge of his bodyguard.

Study Questions

1. How many groups of warriors are mentioned in this passage? Why do you think the Chronicles writer distinguishes them from one another?

_____

_____

_____

_____

2. How were all the men listed in this passage similar to David? What qualities, abilities, and experiences did they have in common?

_____

_____

_____

_____

3. When you read about the exploits of David's mighty men, how do you respond emotionally and intellectually? What is God communicating to you personally as a leader?

_____

_____

_____

_____

3 Evil Follows Evil

1 Kings 21:1–16, 25

¹ Some time later there was an incident involving a vineyard belonging to Naboth the Jezreelite. The vineyard was in Jezreel, close to the palace of Ahab king of Samaria. ² Ahab said to Naboth, "Let me have your vineyard to use for a vegetable garden, since it is close to my palace. In exchange I will give you a better vineyard or, if you prefer, I will pay you whatever it is worth."

³ But Naboth replied, "The LORD forbid that I should give you the inheritance of my ancestors."

⁴ So Ahab went home, sullen and angry because Naboth the Jezreelite had said, "I will not give you the inheritance of my ancestors." He lay on his bed sulking and refused to eat.

⁵ His wife Jezebel came in and asked him, "Why are you so sullen? Why won't you eat?"

⁶ He answered her, "Because I said to Naboth the Jezreelite, 'Sell me your vineyard; or if you prefer, I will give you another vineyard in its place.' But he said, 'I will not give you my vineyard.'"

⁷ Jezebel his wife said, "Is this how you act as king over Israel? Get up and eat! Cheer up. I'll get you the vineyard of Naboth the Jezreelite."

⁸ So she wrote letters in Ahab's name, placed his seal on them, and sent them to the elders and nobles who lived in Naboth's city with him. ⁹ In those letters she wrote:

"Proclaim a day of fasting and seat Naboth in a prominent place among the people. ¹⁰ But seat two scoundrels opposite him and have them bring charges that he has cursed both God and the king. Then take him out and stone him to death."

¹¹ So the elders and nobles who lived in Naboth's city did as Jezebel directed in the letters she had written to them. ¹² They proclaimed a fast and seated Naboth in a prominent place among the people. ¹³ Then two scoundrels came and sat opposite him and brought charges against Naboth before the people, saying, "Naboth has cursed both God and the king." So they took him outside the city and stoned him to death. ¹⁴ Then they sent word to Jezebel: "Naboth has been stoned to death."

¹⁵ As soon as Jezebel heard that Naboth had been stoned to death, she said to Ahab, "Get up and take possession of the vineyard of Naboth the Jezreelite that he refused to sell you. He is no longer alive, but dead." ¹⁶ When Ahab heard that Naboth was dead, he got up and went down to take possession of Naboth's vineyard. . . .

²⁵ (There was never anyone like Ahab, who sold himself to do evil in the eyes of the LORD, urged on by Jezebel his wife.)

Study Questions

1. Do you think Ahab gave Naboth a fair offer for his vineyard? What do you think of Ahab's response to Naboth's refusal? What does it say about Ahab's character?

_____

_____

_____

_____

_____

2. It could be said that Ahab and Jezebel were two of a kind and deserved each other. Which of them was worse? Explain.

_____

_____

_____

_____

_____

3. Why do you think the elders and nobles of Jezreel complied with the letters Jezebel sent to them in Ahab's name?

_____

_____

_____

_____

_____

4. After Ahab took possession of Naboth's vineyard, Elijah the prophet confronted him and prophesied against him and Jezebel. Why do you believe God allows evil leaders to cause the destruction they do?

_____

_____

_____

_____

_____

LEADERSHIP INSIGHT AND REFLECTION

What roles do character, reputation, and proximity play in the Law of Magnetism?

_____

_____

_____

Examine the people closest to you to whom you have been attracted: team members, friends and close associates, and, if married, your spouse. List their names below. Next to each name, describe their character and reputation.

_____

_____

_____

_____

_____

_____

What do they have in common? Which things do you like and admire about them? Which give you cause for concern?

_____

_____

_____

_____

TAKING ACTION

For any characteristic that gave you concern in those around you, examine yourself for those same traits. How do those same characteristics manifest themselves in _you_? What action can you take to improve in that area? Whom can you ask to help you in this area? Whom can you ask to hold you accountable for improvement?

_____

_____

_____

_____

GROUP DISCUSSION QUESTIONS

1. Who was the greater leader: Moses who confronted Pharaoh and led the Israelites out of Egypt, or Joshua who took the people into the Promised Land and settled them there? Explain your answer.

2. How much of Joshua's leadership ability do you think was innate, and how much was influenced and instilled by Moses?

3. What role do you think David's mighty men had in his success?

4. After being confronted by the prophet Elijah, Ahab "went around meekly" (1 Kings 21:27). Do you think Ahab changed internally? What must a person do to truly change after doing wrong?

5. How is your current leadership being impacted by the people in your life?

6. What kinds of changes do you need to make to yourself to improve? Do you also need to change members of your team or your circle of friends? Explain.

7. What change are you willing to make beginning today? Who will you ask to hold you accountable?

THE LAW OF CONNECTION

Leaders Touch a Heart Before
They Ask for a Hand

DEFINITION OF THE LAW

People in leadership communicate in a variety of ways. Some lecture. Others bark orders. Some assume their people already know what to do. And others hide out in their office, refusing to communicate until followers track them down and ask directly.

The above communication styles are unproductive. And they all have one thing in common: a failure to connect. For leaders to be effective and move the team forward, they need to connect with people. Why? Because you first have to touch people's hearts before you ask them for a hand. That is the Law of Connection. If you want your followers on your side, don't try to convince them—connect with them. You can't move people to action unless you first move them with emotion.

I used to tell my staff, "People don't care how much you know until they know how much you care." They would groan because they heard me say it so much, but they recognized that it was true nonetheless. The best way to develop credibility with your employees is to connect with them and show that you genuinely care. When you do that, they are usually more willing to listen to you, learn from you, and make things happen for you. Here are some of the best ways to connect:

Be relational, not positional: Barking orders is positional. It assumes that your employees will rush to obey simply because you're in charge. But remember, leadership is influence. And people will ultimately follow you because they want to. Learn their names, find out who they are outside of work, and figure out what they're good at. Be tuned into their culture, background, education, etc. Then adapt your communication to them personally; don't expect them to adapt to you. The better you know and express care for them as individuals, the more likely they are to want to help you.

Take the first step: Many leaders assume that connecting is the responsibility of followers. They think, *I'm the boss. It's their job to find out what I want. Let them come to me.* But effective leaders are initiators. They don't wait for their people to seek them out or ask questions. They make the effort to connect and offer guidance first, which empowers and encourages the team.

Listen and learn who they are and what they want: Communication is about more than the message. You need to know your audience and meet them where they are. Start by focusing on them more than yourself. Ask questions and listen, with the goal of discovering what they desire and dream about. Then you can speak to what they care about, not just what you care about.

Be authentic and offer real help: Don't *act* caring. *Be* caring. Believe in your people's value. And practice what you preach. When your words accurately represent who you are, what you believe, and how you act, you gain credibility with your team. And people want to partner with a leader they believe in.

People truly don't care how much you know until they know how much you care. Don't underestimate the importance of building relational bridges between yourself and your followers. There's an old saying: to lead yourself, use your head; to lead others, use your heart. That's the nature of the Law of Connection. Always touch a person's heart before you ask for a hand.

CASE STUDIES

Read these case studies from the Bible and answer the study questions that follow.

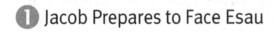 Jacob Prepares to Face Esau

Genesis 32:3–12

³ Jacob sent messengers ahead of him to his brother Esau in the land of Seir, the country of Edom. ⁴ He instructed them: "This is what you are to say to my lord Esau:

'Your servant Jacob says, I have been staying with Laban and have remained there till now. ⁵ I have cattle and donkeys, sheep and goats, male and female servants. Now I am sending this message to my lord, that I may find favor in your eyes.'"

⁶ When the messengers returned to Jacob, they said, "We went to your brother Esau, and now he is coming to meet you, and four hundred men are with him."

⁷ In great fear and distress Jacob divided the people who were with him into two groups, and the flocks and herds and camels as well. ⁸ He thought, "If Esau comes and attacks one group, the group that is left may escape."

⁹ Then Jacob prayed, "O God of my father Abraham, God of my father Isaac, Lord, you who said to me, 'Go back to your country and your relatives, and I will make you prosper,' ¹⁰ I am unworthy of all the kindness and faithfulness you have shown your servant. I had only my staff when I crossed this Jordan, but now I have become two camps. ¹¹ Save me, I pray, from the hand of my brother Esau, for I am afraid he will come and attack me, and also the mothers with their children. ¹² But you have said, 'I will surely make you prosper and will make your descendants like the sand of the sea, which cannot be counted.'"

Genesis 33:1–11

¹ Jacob looked up and there was Esau, coming with his four hundred men; so he divided the children among Leah, Rachel and the two female servants. ² He put the female servants and their children in front, Leah and her children next, and Rachel and Joseph in the rear. ³ He himself went on ahead and bowed down to the ground seven times as he approached his brother.

⁴ But Esau ran to meet Jacob and embraced him; he threw his arms around his neck and kissed him. And they wept. ⁵ Then Esau looked up and saw the women and children. "Who are these with you?" he asked.

Jacob answered, "They are the children God has graciously given your servant." ⁶ Then the female servants and their children approached and bowed down. ⁷ Next, Leah and her children came and bowed down. Last of all came Joseph and Rachel, and they too bowed down.

⁸ Esau asked, "What's the meaning of all these flocks and herds I met?"

"To find favor in your eyes, my lord," he said.

⁹ But Esau said, "I already have plenty, my brother. Keep what you have for yourself."

[10] *"No, please!" said Jacob. "If I have found favor in your eyes, accept this gift from me. For to see your face is like seeing the face of God, now that you have received me favorably. [11] Please accept the present that was brought to you, for God has been gracious to me and I have all I need." And because Jacob insisted, Esau accepted it.*

Study Questions

1. Review the passages carefully. What did Jacob do to connect with Esau? Make a list here.

_____

_____

_____

_____

_____

_____

_____

2. When Jacob left home twenty years before, he was on bad terms with his brother Esau, whom he had tricked out of his birthright. Was Jacob's preparation to meet his twin brother more trickery or leadership wisdom? Explain.

_____

_____

_____

_____

_____

_____

3. What do you think would have turned out differently if Jacob had done nothing to connect with Esau? Explain.

_____

_____

_____

_____

_____

2 Absalom Uses Connection for Self-Promotion

2 Samuel 15:1–13

¹ In the course of time, [King David's son] Absalom provided himself with a chariot and horses and with fifty men to run ahead of him. ² He would get up early and stand by the side of the road leading to the city gate. Whenever anyone came with a complaint to be placed before the king for a decision, Absalom would call out to him, "What town are you from?" He would answer, "Your servant is from one of the tribes of Israel." ³ Then Absalom would say to him, "Look, your claims are valid and proper, but there is no representative of the king to hear you." ⁴ And Absalom would add, "If only I were appointed judge in the land! Then everyone who has a complaint or case could come to me and I would see that they receive justice."

⁵ Also, whenever anyone approached him to bow down before him, Absalom would reach out his hand, take hold of him and kiss him. ⁶ Absalom behaved in this way toward all the Israelites who came to the king asking for justice, and so he stole the hearts of the people of Israel.

⁷ At the end of four years, Absalom said to the king, "Let me go to Hebron and fulfill a vow I made to the LORD. ⁸ While your servant was living at Geshur in Aram, I made this vow: 'If the LORD takes me back to Jerusalem, I will worship the LORD in Hebron.'"

⁹ The king said to him, "Go in peace." So he went to Hebron.

¹⁰ Then Absalom sent secret messengers throughout the tribes of Israel to say, "As soon as you hear the sound of the trumpets, then say, 'Absalom is king in Hebron.'" ¹¹ Two hundred men from Jerusalem had accompanied Absalom. They had been invited as guests and went quite innocently, knowing nothing about the matter. ¹² While Absalom was offering sacrifices, he also sent for Ahithophel the Gilonite, David's counselor, to come from Giloh, his hometown. And so the conspiracy gained strength, and Absalom's following kept on increasing.

¹³ A messenger came and told David, "The hearts of the people of Israel are with Absalom."

Study Questions

1. What kinds of people did Absalom appeal to, and what steps did he take to connect with them?

   _____

   _____

   _____

   _____

2. Do you believe Absalom's self-serving motives positively or negatively impacted his ability to connect with others? Explain.

   _____

   _____

   _____

   _____

3. Do you think the people on the road to Jerusalem cared about Absalom's motives? What emotions do leaders appeal to when they are trying to manipulate people? How can people best discern any leader's motivations?

   _____

   _____

   _____

   _____

   _____

③ Paul Connects Instead of Commanding

Philemon 1:1–21

¹ Paul, a prisoner of Christ Jesus, and Timothy our brother,
   To Philemon our dear friend and fellow worker— ² also to Apphia our sister and Archippus our fellow soldier—and to the church that meets in your home:

³ Grace and peace to you from God our Father and the Lord Jesus Christ.

⁴ I always thank my God as I remember you in my prayers, ⁵ because I hear about your love for all his holy people and your faith in the Lord Jesus. ⁶ I pray that your partnership with us in the faith may be effective in deepening your understanding of every good thing we share for the sake of Christ. ⁷ Your love has given me great joy and encouragement, because you, brother, have refreshed the hearts of the Lord's people.

⁸ Therefore, although in Christ I could be bold and order you to do what you ought to do, ⁹ yet I prefer to appeal to you on the basis of love. It is as none other than Paul—an old man and now also a prisoner of Christ Jesus— ¹⁰ that I appeal to you for my son Onesimus, who became my son while I was in chains. ¹¹ Formerly he was useless to you, but now he has become useful both to you and to me.

¹² I am sending him—who is my very heart—back to you. ¹³ I would have liked to keep him with me so that he could take your place in helping me while I am in chains for the gospel. ¹⁴ But I did not want to do anything without your consent, so that any favor you do would not seem forced but would be voluntary. ¹⁵ Perhaps the reason he was separated from you for a little while was that you might have him back forever— ¹⁶ no longer as a slave, but better than a slave, as a dear brother. He is very dear to me but even dearer to you, both as a fellow man and as a brother in the Lord.

¹⁷ So if you consider me a partner, welcome him as you would welcome me. ¹⁸ If he has done you any wrong or owes you anything, charge it to me. ¹⁹ I, Paul, am writing this with my own hand. I will pay it back—not to mention that you owe me your very self. ²⁰ I do wish, brother, that I may have some benefit from you in the Lord; refresh my heart in Christ. ²¹ Confident of your obedience, I write to you, knowing that you will do even more than I ask.

Study Questions

1. What things did Paul write in order to connect with Philemon?

_____

_____

_____

_____

2. What were Paul's motives for writing this letter?

_____

_____

_____

_____

_____

3. Why do you think Paul chose to connect with Philemon instead of command him? Would you have been persuaded? Explain.

_____

_____

_____

_____

_____

4. What is the long-term effect of connecting and appealing to someone's higher motivations?

_____

_____

_____

_____

_____

LEADERSHIP INSIGHT AND REFLECTION

Think about the three leaders who used the Law of Connection in these passages. How powerful a leadership skill is touching someone's heart before asking for a hand? Why?

_____

_____

_____

_____

_____

_____

Which best describes you:

- I'm not a people person, so I don't really try to connect with people.
- I like to connect with people, but I wait for them to initiate.
- I connect with people when it serves my purpose.
- I connect with the people I lead for our mutual benefit.
- I try to connect with everyone.

Explain why you chose your answer.

_____
_____
_____
_____

TAKING ACTION

Think about your answer to the last question. If you answered anything other than the final two response options, you have work to do, either in your willingness to connect with people or in your motives. Keeping in mind that 1 John 4:20 says, "Whoever claims to love God yet hates a brother or sister is a liar," what must you do to change?

_____
_____
_____
_____
_____

What tangible step will you take this week to begin connecting better with others?

_____
_____
_____
_____
_____

GROUP DISCUSSION QUESTIONS

1. What were the stakes for Jacob, Absalom, and Paul as they tried to connect in the passages you read?

2. The passage says Absalom met people on the road for four years. What is your reaction to that?

3. What groundwork had Paul already laid with Philemon before he wrote the letter to him on behalf of Onesimus? How important do you think that history was?

4. Do you regularly try to connect with the people you lead? If so, how?

5. When does connecting no longer become necessary with the people you lead?

6. What was your greatest takeaway from this lesson?

7. What changes in your leadership do you believe God is asking you to make as a result of this lesson? How do you intend to change and when will you take action?

THE LAW OF THE INNER CIRCLE

A Leader's Potential Is Determined by Those Closest to Him

DEFINITION OF THE LAW

Whenever we see incredibly accomplished people, it's easy to believe that they got to where they are all by themselves. We often want to give them all the credit. But to think that way is to buy in to a lie. Nothing truly great or impactful was achieved by one person alone. This is especially true of leaders. For a leader to achieve at all—or even be considered a leader—he or she needs a team. Together, they can make an impact. How much of an impact depends on who is on the team—and especially those in the inner circle. A leader's potential is determined by those closest to him or her. That's the Law of the Inner Circle.

Most of us naturally gather an inner circle—the small group of people we trust and spend the most time with. However, we're not always strategic about it. We tend to surround ourselves with either those we like or people with whom we are comfortable. But we don't always think about how each one might impact our effectiveness or leadership potential. You see it all the time among famous athletes and entertainers. Some, in spite of great talent or gifting, never seem to reach their potential. Others actually self-destruct, making decisions that cost them their careers or their financial security. Often, these mistakes can be attributed to the kinds of people they spend most of their time with.

To practice the Law of the Inner Circle, you must be intentional about who you allow into that group. Who should you trust the most and spend the most time with? The people in a leader's inner circle need to represent the leader well, make the leader better, or both.

First, they should be trustworthy. If they're going to represent or influence you, they should demonstrate excellence, maturity, and good character in everything they do. If their track record over time doesn't show these qualities, remove them from the list of candidates.

Next, they should add value to you and the team. A team consists of individuals who contribute at every level. The people you invite into your inner circle should have a proven track record as assets, both to the organization and to you personally. If they subtract more than they add, they don't belong in the inner circle.

Your inner circle should include people who have high influence with others. Influencers can carry your vision and values to the rest of the team and beyond. They can also make you better as a leader, as you ask for their input and listen to their advice.

You also need people whose gifts complement yours. Leaders can't be strong in every area. Don't fill your team with people just like you. Instead, include individuals in your inner circle who are gifted where you are not. They will allow you to focus your time and energy on your areas of strength. Plus, their unique perspective will give you insights that you might have missed on your own.

Include those who occupy a strategic position on the team. You and they must be on the same page, or the entire organization could be in trouble. Members of the inner circle know what you're thinking better and sooner than everyone else. Key players should be in the room when those big decisions are made, so they know right away how to implement them.

Seek for your inner circle people who get along and help you and each other improve. Solomon of ancient Israel recognized this truth when he wrote, "As iron sharpens iron, friends sharpen the minds of each other." If your inner circle is going to function as a team, then you need to ensure they have a good fit and raise one another's game.

You'll probably discover some potential candidates who aren't quite ready to join the inner circle, but they could be with some help from you. These people have great potential, so invest your time and energy into developing them.

If you want to increase your capacity and maximize your potential as a leader, your first step is always to become the best leader you can be. The next is to surround yourself with the best leaders you can find. Never forget that a leader's potential is determined by those closest to him or her. That's the Law of the Inner Circle. That's the only way you and your team can reach the highest level possible.

CASE STUDIES

Read these case studies from the Bible and answer the study questions that follow.

① Abraham's Trusted Servant

Genesis 24:1–27

[1] Abraham was now very old, and the LORD had blessed him in every way. [2] He said to the senior servant in his household, the one in charge of all that he had, "Put your hand under my thigh. [3] I want you to swear by the LORD, the God of heaven and the God of earth, that you will not get a wife for my son from the daughters of the Canaanites, among whom I am living, [4] but will go to my country and my own relatives and get a wife for my son Isaac."

[5] The servant asked him, "What if the woman is unwilling to come back with me to this land? Shall I then take your son back to the country you came from?"

[6] "Make sure that you do not take my son back there," Abraham said. [7] "The LORD, the God of heaven, who brought me out of my father's household and my native land and who spoke to me and promised me on oath, saying, 'To your offspring I will give this land'—he will send his angel before you so that you can get a wife for my son from there. [8] If the woman is unwilling to come back with you, then you will be released from this oath of mine. Only do not take my son back there." [9] So the servant put his hand under the thigh of his master Abraham and swore an oath to him concerning this matter.

[10] Then the servant left, taking with him ten of his master's camels loaded with all kinds of good things from his master. He set out for Aram Naharaim and made his way to the town of Nahor. [11] He had the camels kneel down near the well outside the town; it was toward evening, the time the women go out to draw water.

[12] Then he prayed, "Lord, God of my master Abraham, make me successful today, and show kindness to my master Abraham. [13] See, I am standing beside this spring, and the daughters of the townspeople are coming out to draw water. [14] May it be that when I say to a young woman, 'Please let down your jar that I may have a drink,' and she says, 'Drink, and I'll water your camels too'—let her be the one you have chosen for your servant Isaac. By this I will know that you have shown kindness to my master."

[15] Before he had finished praying, Rebekah came out with her jar on her shoulder. She was the daughter of Bethuel son of Milkah, who was the wife of Abraham's brother Nahor. [16] The woman was very beautiful, a virgin; no man had ever slept with her. She went down to the spring, filled her jar and came up again.

[17] The servant hurried to meet her and said, "Please give me a little water from your jar."

[18] "Drink, my lord," she said, and quickly lowered the jar to her hands and gave him a drink.

[19] After she had given him a drink, she said, "I'll draw water for your camels too, until they have had enough to drink." [20] So she quickly emptied her jar into the trough, ran back to the well to draw more water, and drew enough for all his camels. [21] Without saying a word, the man watched her closely to learn whether or not the Lord had made his journey successful.

[22] When the camels had finished drinking, the man took out a gold nose ring weighing a beka and two gold bracelets weighing ten shekels. [23] Then he asked, "Whose daughter are you? Please tell me, is there room in your father's house for us to spend the night?"

[24] She answered him, "I am the daughter of Bethuel, the son that Milkah bore to Nahor." [25] And she added, "We have plenty of straw and fodder, as well as room for you to spend the night."

[26] Then the man bowed down and worshiped the Lord, [27] saying, "Praise be to the Lord, the God of my master Abraham, who has not abandoned his

kindness and faithfulness to my master. As for me, the LORD has led me on the journey to the house of my master's relatives."

Study Questions

1. What does it say about the relationship between Abraham and the senior servant that the man was sent to find a wife for Isaac?

_____

_____

_____

_____

_____

2. Why do you think Abraham didn't send his son Isaac to Aram himself to find a wife?

_____

_____

_____

_____

3. Why was it so important to Abraham that Isaac not marry a Canaanite woman? How would Isaac's marriage relate to the Law of the Inner Circle?

_____

_____

_____

_____

_____

② Leveraging the Law of the Inner Circle

2 Samuel 15:32–34

32 When David arrived at the summit, where people used to worship God, Hushai the Arkite was there to meet him, his robe torn and dust on his head. *33* David said to him, "If you go with me, you will be a burden to me. *34* But if you return to the city and say to Absalom, 'Your Majesty, I will be your servant; I was your father's servant in the past, but now I will be your servant,' then you can help me by frustrating Ahithophel's advice."

2 Samuel 17:1–16

1 Ahithophel said to Absalom, "I would choose twelve thousand men and set out tonight in pursuit of David. *2* I would attack him while he is weary and weak. I would strike him with terror, and then all the people with him will flee. I would strike down only the king *3* and bring all the people back to you. The death of the man you seek will mean the return of all; all the people will be unharmed." *4* This plan seemed good to Absalom and to all the elders of Israel.

5 But Absalom said, "Summon also Hushai the Arkite, so we can hear what he has to say as well." *6* When Hushai came to him, Absalom said, "Ahithophel has given this advice. Should we do what he says? If not, give us your opinion."

7 Hushai replied to Absalom, "The advice Ahithophel has given is not good this time. *8* You know your father and his men; they are fighters, and as fierce as a wild bear robbed of her cubs. Besides, your father is an experienced fighter; he will not spend the night with the troops. *9* Even now, he is hidden in a cave or some other place. If he should attack your troops first, whoever hears about it will say, 'There has been a slaughter among the troops who follow Absalom.' *10* Then even the bravest soldier, whose heart is like the heart of a lion, will melt with fear, for all Israel knows that your father is a fighter and that those with him are brave.

11 "So I advise you: Let all Israel, from Dan to Beersheba—as numerous as the sand on the seashore—be gathered to you, with you yourself leading them into battle. *12* Then we will attack him wherever he may be found, and we will fall on him as dew settles on the ground. Neither he nor any of his men will be left alive. *13* If he withdraws into a city, then all Israel will bring ropes to that city, and we will drag it down to the valley until not so much as a pebble is left."

14 Absalom and all the men of Israel said, "The advice of Hushai the Arkite is better than that of Ahithophel." For the Lord had determined to frustrate the good advice of Ahithophel in order to bring disaster on Absalom.

¹⁵ *Hushai told Zadok and Abiathar, the priests, "Ahithophel has advised Absalom and the elders of Israel to do such and such, but I have advised them to do so and so. ¹⁶ Now send a message at once and tell David, 'Do not spend the night at the fords in the wilderness; cross over without fail, or the king and all the people with him will be swallowed up.'"*

Study Questions

1. What was David's opinion of Ahithophel?

_____

_____

_____

_____

_____

_____

_____

2. How well did David understand the Law of the Inner Circle? How well did Absalom?

_____

_____

_____

_____

_____

_____

_____

3. What do you think would have happened if Absalom had taken Ahithophel's advice?

_____

_____

_____

_____

_____

_____

4. When leaders have more than one wise adviser in their inner circle, how can they discern whose advice to take?

_____

_____

_____

_____

③ A Hard Truth

2 Samuel 12:1–13

[1] The LORD sent Nathan to David. When he came to him, he said, "There were two men in a certain town, one rich and the other poor. [2] The rich man had a very large number of sheep and cattle, [3] but the poor man had nothing except one little ewe lamb he had bought. He raised it, and it grew up with him and his children. It shared his food, drank from his cup and even slept in his arms. It was like a daughter to him.

[4] "Now a traveler came to the rich man, but the rich man refrained from taking one of his own sheep or cattle to prepare a meal for the traveler who had come to him. Instead, he took the ewe lamb that belonged to the poor man and prepared it for the one who had come to him."

[5] David burned with anger against the man and said to Nathan, "As surely as the LORD lives, the man who did this must die! [6] He must pay for that lamb four times over, because he did such a thing and had no pity."

[7] Then Nathan said to David, "You are the man! This is what the LORD, the God of Israel, says: 'I anointed you king over Israel, and I delivered you from the hand of Saul. [8] I gave your master's house to you, and your master's wives into your arms. I gave you all Israel and Judah. And if all this had been too little, I would have given you even more. [9] Why did you despise the word of the LORD by doing what is evil in his eyes? You struck down Uriah the Hittite with the sword and took his wife to be your own. You killed him with the sword of the Ammonites. [10] Now, therefore, the

sword will never depart from your house, because you despised me and took the wife of Uriah the Hittite to be your own.'

[11] *"This is what the Lord says: 'Out of your own household I am going to bring calamity on you. Before your very eyes I will take your wives and give them to one who is close to you, and he will sleep with your wives in broad daylight.* [12] *You did it in secret, but I will do this thing in broad daylight before all Israel.'"*

[13] *Then David said to Nathan, "I have sinned against the Lord."*

Study Questions

1. How difficult do you think it was for Nathan the prophet to confront King David?

_____

_____

_____

_____

_____

_____

2. Why did Nathan use a story to communicate with David rather than just confronting him directly in the beginning about Uriah and his wife, Bathsheba?

_____

_____

_____

_____

3. What does David's response to the confrontation say about him as a person and as a leader?

_____

_____

_____

_____

_____

LEADERSHIP INSIGHT AND REFLECTION

Based on the passages you read, what are the benefits of an inner circle?

_____
_____
_____
_____
_____
_____

What are the potential dangers of an inner circle?

_____
_____
_____
_____
_____

Write down the names of the people in your inner circle—the family members, friends, team members, colleagues, mentors, and advisers who influence your thinking and actions. Next to their names, write how they influence you. Place a plus beside the ones who add value to you and a minus beside those who are not a clearly positive influence. (Do not consider anyone neutral. If someone seems neutral, think until you find something positive or negative.)

_____
_____
_____
_____
_____
_____
_____
_____
_____

Evaluate your list. Are there more positives or negatives? If there are many negatives, try to determine why you are attracting and embracing negative people in your life.

TAKING ACTION

Your goal in life should be to surround yourself with people who are a positive influence on you and your leadership (enabling you to become a positive influence in the lives of others). What can you do to insulate yourself from negative influences and seek out more positive influences to bring into your inner circle?

_____
_____
_____
_____
_____
_____
_____
_____
_____
_____
_____
_____
_____
_____
_____

GROUP DISCUSSION QUESTIONS

1. Was the result of Abraham sending his servant to find Isaac a wife luck, faith, or strategic leadership? Explain.

2. How do you think David felt when Absalom rebelled against him and tried to take the throne? Would you have been inclined to be strategic as David was and fight Absalom, or to become demoralized and give up? Explain.

3. What kinds of advice did members of the inner circle give their leaders in the stories?

4. Why do you believe David was open to Nathan's input? What made him willing to listen and respond as he did?

5. Who have you given permission to speak into your life the way Nathan did to David? How do you typically respond?

6. What was your greatest takeaway about the Law of the Inner Circle from this lesson?

7. What action do you believe God is asking you to take related to your inner circle as a result of this lesson? When and how will you do it?

THE LAW OF EMPOWERMENT

Only Secure Leaders Give Power to Others

DEFINITION OF THE LAW

After influencing people to follow, effective leaders guide and empower those followers. Guidance tells people where to go and what to do. Empowerment gives them the tools and ability to get there. When leaders offer resources and authority, they clear the path between followers and the assigned goal. When the people are empowered, they are able to both do the job and reach their full potential. And everyone wins.

When leaders assign responsibility without providing resources or authority, they undermine rather than empower. And the path to the goal is blocked with huge barriers followers must struggle to overcome. Sometimes they do reach the goal, but only with great effort. The organization and the leader might win in the short term, but the team members feel like they've lost. And if they constantly face obstacles left or placed by the leader, people either give up and stop trying, or they leave. People want to follow leaders who allow and equip them to succeed and maximize their potential.

Unfortunately, this is a common problem. But why would a leader make it difficult for followers to succeed? Why are so many leaders either unable or unwilling to empower their people? Because of insecurity. Insecurity creates its own barriers that the leader must overcome in order to empower his or her people. Here are some of those barriers to empowerment:

Craving for job security: Insecure leaders worry that if they help subordinates, they themselves will become dispensable. But the reality is that when you consistently empower others and help them develop enough that they could take over your job, you will become so valuable to the organization that you are indispensable. You will develop a pattern of achievement, excellence, and leadership. If your teams always seem to succeed, people will figure out that you are leading them well.

Resistance to change: Empowerment is a source of constant change, because when you grant authority, you allow your people to make their own decisions, which are probably different from yours. That can be nerve-racking because it means giving up control. Yet by giving team members free rein in how they achieve the goal, you enable them to develop creativity and problem-solving skills. They also feel pride in their accomplishment. And the organization benefits from new and better ways of thinking. To empower is to become a change agent.

Lack of self-worth: Empowering leaders believe in their people because they believe in themselves. They see themselves as works in progress and are comfortable with mistakes. This sense of personal security gives them confidence to accept responsibility and authority for their role. And it enables them to entrust their people with authority and give them credit for what they accomplish.

Empowering leaders remove all the barriers between the team and the goal, because they believe in themselves, their mission, and their people. Only secure leaders give power to others. And empowerment is powerful—for both followers and leaders. Enlarging others makes you larger. That is the impact of the Law of Empowerment. It is an impact you can experience as a leader as long as you are willing to believe in people and give your power away.

CASE STUDIES

Read these case studies from the Bible and answer the study questions that follow.

 **Moses the One-Man Band**

Exodus 18:13–26

13 The next day Moses took his seat to serve as judge for the people, and they stood around him from morning till evening. 14 When his father-in-law saw all that Moses was doing for the people, he said, "What is this you are doing for the people? Why do you alone sit as judge, while all these people stand around you from morning till evening?"

¹⁵ Moses answered him, "Because the people come to me to seek God's will. ¹⁶ Whenever they have a dispute, it is brought to me, and I decide between the parties and inform them of God's decrees and instructions."

¹⁷ Moses' father-in-law replied, "What you are doing is not good. ¹⁸ You and these people who come to you will only wear yourselves out. The work is too heavy for you; you cannot handle it alone. ¹⁹ Listen now to me and I will give you some advice, and may God be with you. You must be the people's representative before God and bring their disputes to him. ²⁰ Teach them his decrees and instructions, and show them the way they are to live and how they are to behave. ²¹ But select capable men from all the people—men who fear God, trustworthy men who hate dishonest gain—and appoint them as officials over thousands, hundreds, fifties and tens. ²² Have them serve as judges for the people at all times, but have them bring every difficult case to you; the simple cases they can decide themselves. That will make your load lighter, because they will share it with you. ²³ If you do this and God so commands, you will be able to stand the strain, and all these people will go home satisfied."

²⁴ Moses listened to his father-in-law and did everything he said. ²⁵ He chose capable men from all Israel and made them leaders of the people, officials over thousands, hundreds, fifties and tens. ²⁶ They served as judges for the people at all times. The difficult cases they brought to Moses, but the simple ones they decided themselves.

Study Questions

1. Why was Moses sitting alone as judge and doing everything himself?

   _____

   _____

   _____

   _____

   _____

2. What do Jethro's observations and advice indicate about his leadership ability?

_____

_____

_____

_____

3. Why do you think Jethro advised Moses to appoint leaders to different groups: thousands, hundreds, fifties, and tens?

_____

_____

_____

_____

4. What made Moses willing and able to implement Jethro's plan?

_____

_____

_____

_____

❷ Ezra is Empowered to Lead

Ezra 7:11–28

¹¹ *This is a copy of the letter King Artaxerxes had given to Ezra the priest, a teacher of the Law, a man learned in matters concerning the commands and decrees of the Lord for Israel:*

> ¹² *Artaxerxes, king of kings,*
>> *To Ezra the priest, teacher of the Law of the God of heaven:*
>> *Greetings.*
>
> ¹³ *Now I decree that any of the Israelites in my kingdom, including priests and Levites, who volunteer to go to Jerusalem with you, may go.* ¹⁴ *You are sent by the king and his seven advisers to inquire about Judah and Jerusalem with regard to the Law of your God, which is in your hand.*

¹⁵ Moreover, you are to take with you the silver and gold that the king and his advisers have freely given to the God of Israel, whose dwelling is in Jerusalem, ¹⁶ together with all the silver and gold you may obtain from the province of Babylon, as well as the freewill offerings of the people and priests for the temple of their God in Jerusalem. ¹⁷ With this money be sure to buy bulls, rams and male lambs, together with their grain offerings and drink offerings, and sacrifice them on the altar of the temple of your God in Jerusalem.

¹⁸ You and your fellow Israelites may then do whatever seems best with the rest of the silver and gold, in accordance with the will of your God. ¹⁹ Deliver to the God of Jerusalem all the articles entrusted to you for worship in the temple of your God. ²⁰ And anything else needed for the temple of your God that you are responsible to supply, you may provide from the royal treasury.

²¹ Now I, King Artaxerxes, decree that all the treasurers of Trans-Euphrates are to provide with diligence whatever Ezra the priest, the teacher of the Law of the God of heaven, may ask of you— ²² up to a hundred talents of silver, a hundred cors of wheat, a hundred baths of wine, a hundred baths of olive oil, and salt without limit. ²³ Whatever the God of heaven has prescribed, let it be done with diligence for the temple of the God of heaven. Why should his wrath fall on the realm of the king and of his sons? ²⁴ You are also to know that you have no authority to impose taxes, tribute or duty on any of the priests, Levites, musicians, gatekeepers, temple servants or other workers at this house of God.

²⁵ And you, Ezra, in accordance with the wisdom of your God, which you possess, appoint magistrates and judges to administer justice to all the people of Trans-Euphrates—all who know the laws of your God. And you are to teach any who do not know them. ²⁶ Whoever does not obey the law of your God and the law of the king must surely be punished by death, banishment, confiscation of property, or imprisonment.

²⁷ Praise be to the LORD, the God of our ancestors, who has put it into the king's heart to bring honor to the house of the LORD in Jerusalem in this way ²⁸ and who has extended his good favor to me before the king and his advisers and all the king's powerful officials. Because the hand of the LORD my God was on me, I took courage and gathered leaders from Israel to go up with me.

Study Questions

1. What were all of the ways Artaxerxes, king of Persia, worked to empower Ezra and set him up for success? List them.

   _____

   _____

   _____

   _____

2. What impact does Ezra say this empowerment had on him?

   _____

   _____

   _____

3. What can you conclude about Artaxerxes as a leader from this passage?

   _____

   _____

   _____

❸ Jesus Empowers and Warns

Matthew 10:1–33

¹ *Jesus called his twelve disciples to him and gave them authority to drive out impure spirits and to heal every disease and sickness.*

² *These are the names of the twelve apostles: first, Simon (who is called Peter) and his brother Andrew; James son of Zebedee, and his brother John;* ³ *Philip and Bartholomew; Thomas and Matthew the tax collector; James son of Alphaeus, and Thaddaeus;* ⁴ *Simon the Zealot and Judas Iscariot, who betrayed him.*

⁵ *These twelve Jesus sent out with the following instructions: "Do not go among the Gentiles or enter any town of the Samaritans.* ⁶ *Go rather to the lost sheep of Israel.* ⁷ *As you go, proclaim this message: 'The kingdom of heaven has come near.'* ⁸ *Heal the sick, raise the dead, cleanse those who have leprosy, drive out demons. Freely you have received; freely give.*

⁹ *"Do not get any gold or silver or copper to take with you in your belts —*
¹⁰ *no bag for the journey or extra shirt or sandals or a staff, for the worker is worth his keep.* ¹¹ *Whatever town or village you enter, search there for some worthy person and stay at their house until you leave.* ¹² *As you enter the home, give it your greeting.* ¹³ *If the home is deserving, let your peace rest on it; if it is not, let your peace return to you.* ¹⁴ *If anyone will not welcome you or listen to your words, leave that home or town and shake the dust off your feet.* ¹⁵ *Truly I tell you, it will be more bearable for Sodom and Gomorrah on the day of judgment than for that town.*

¹⁶ *"I am sending you out like sheep among wolves. Therefore be as shrewd as snakes and as innocent as doves.* ¹⁷ *Be on your guard; you will be handed over to the local councils and be flogged in the synagogues.* ¹⁸ *On my account you will be brought before governors and kings as witnesses to them and to the Gentiles.* ¹⁹ *But when they arrest you, do not worry about what to say or how to say it. At that time you will be given what to say,* ²⁰ *for it will not be you speaking, but the Spirit of your Father speaking through you.*

²¹ *"Brother will betray brother to death, and a father his child; children will rebel against their parents and have them put to death.* ²² *You will be hated by everyone because of me, but the one who stands firm to the end will be saved.* ²³ *When you are persecuted in one place, flee to another. Truly I tell you, you will not finish going through the towns of Israel before the Son of Man comes.*

²⁴ *"The student is not above the teacher, nor a servant above his master.* ²⁵ *It is enough for students to be like their teachers, and servants like their masters. If the head of the house has been called Beelzebul, how much more the members of his household!*

²⁶ *"So do not be afraid of them, for there is nothing concealed that will not be disclosed, or hidden that will not be made known.* ²⁷ *What I tell you in the dark, speak in the daylight; what is whispered in your ear, proclaim from the roofs.* ²⁸ *Do not be afraid of those who kill the body but cannot kill the soul. Rather, be afraid of the One who can destroy both soul and body in hell.* ²⁹ *Are not two sparrows sold for a penny? Yet not one of them will fall to the ground outside your Father's care.* ³⁰ *And even the very hairs of your head are all numbered.* ³¹ *So don't be afraid; you are worth more than many sparrows.*

³² *"Whoever acknowledges me before others, I will also acknowledge before my Father in heaven.* ³³ *But whoever disowns me before others, I will disown before my Father in heaven.*

Study Questions

1. What specific authority did Jesus give to his twelve disciples?

   _____

   _____

   _____

   _____

2. What responsibilities did Jesus give them?

   _____

   _____

   _____

3. Why do you think Jesus told them not to take extra money, clothes, or supplies with them as he sent them out?

   _____

   _____

   _____

4. Why do you think Jesus warned them about the negative things that would happen to his followers? What does that indicate about Jesus' leadership?

   _____

   _____

   _____

LEADERSHIP INSIGHT AND REFLECTION

What was the motivation for each of the leaders in these passages to delegate? Was the authority they gave to others empowering or not? Explain.

_____

_____

_____

_____

_____

What authority do you need to give others to empower them to be more effective? Have you been giving it? Explain?

_____

_____

_____

_____

If you have not been empowering others effectively, what has been the cause of the breakdown? Circle all that apply.

- Lack of confidence in the people you lead
- Past failures or mistakes by the people to whom you delegate
- Insecurity about being overshadowed or displaced
- Uncertainty about how to delegate
- Lack of authority to delegate

What does your answer indicate about where you need to grow and change?

_____

_____

_____

_____

TAKING ACTION

Think about your answer to the last question. What specific action can you take to overcome your biggest problem in delegating to others and empowering them? When will you do it?

_____

_____

_____

_____

_____

Group Discussion Questions

1. If you had been in Moses' position, how would you have responded to Jethro's criticism?

2. Jethro's system worked for Moses. How do you think it also set up the Israelites for success in the future?

3. Why do you think Artaxerxes did what he did for Ezra and the Israelites?

4. If you had been one of the disciples, what would have been your response to Jesus' instructions? Would you have been more thrilled by the power he was giving or more frightened by the challenges you would face?

5. Have you ever experienced a time when you sensed that God was giving you something difficult and important to do? How did you respond? What did you learn?

6. What was your greatest takeaway from this lesson?

7. What changes in your leadership do you believe God is asking you to make so that you become a more empowering leader? What action do you intend to take, and when will you do it? If you need someone's help to follow through, who will you seek out, and how could that person help?

THE LAW OF THE PICTURE

People Do What People See

DEFINITION OF THE LAW

Leaders are stewards of the big picture. They are responsible for the vision they have for the present and future of the team or organization. But while it's clear in their eyes, it appears fuzzy to their followers. Effective leaders consistently *share* the big picture to help followers *understand* it. But even more important, they must consistently *live* it out if they want followers to *act* on it. Because people do what people see. That's the Law of the Picture.

Most leaders spend a lot of time speaking or writing about the big picture—the long-term goal—and that's important. It needs to be communicated both clearly and creatively. But communication is more than words. Describing what you want people to do is not enough. You must also demonstrate it. Effective modeling is what brings the picture into focus and convinces followers to pursue it with you.

What people see is what they will believe. And followers are always watching. If you are a parent, you know that your children are always watching you. Ultimately, it doesn't matter what you tell them—your children believe what they see you do. It's the same with leaders and followers. Followers will compare the leader's words with their actions. And they will always believe the leader's behavior represents what they value, far more than what they say.

What people see is what they will do. That's why it's more important to do what you want done than to teach what you want done. After all, it doesn't matter how many times parents (and bosses) say, "Do as I say, not as I do"—it doesn't work. People want to follow a leader who's been there, done that. Too many leaders are like bad travel agents. They try to send followers to places where they have never been. Instead, the best leaders are like tour guides, taking their people along on the journey and leading by example. They still verbally guide their followers and hold them accountable. But they also provide an obvious model for followers to emulate.

What people see is what they will remember. Not only does the big picture start out unclear to followers, it loses clarity over time. The picture fades when people are not reminded of it over and over again. Again, effective leaders share the long-term goals verbally all the time. But they never stop there. To keep your people continually focused on the big picture, you must consistently act on it yourself. To keep the picture on people's minds, so that they will act on it, leaders must demonstrate it daily.

Consistent modeling of the picture requires good self-leadership. Doing the right thing day after day is neither natural nor easy. But it's essential, so you must start by constantly reminding yourself of the big picture. Compare it to your actions. And hold yourself accountable and learn from your mistakes. Only when the leader's actions line up with the big picture does it become a reality. People do what people see. That is the Law of the Picture.

CASE STUDIES

Read these case studies from the Bible and answer the study questions that follow.

1 Josiah—A King Like No Other

2 Kings 23:1–16, 24–25

¹ Then the king called together all the elders of Judah and Jerusalem. ² He went up to the temple of the LORD with the people of Judah, the inhabitants of Jerusalem, the priests and the prophets—all the people from the least to the greatest. He read in their hearing all the words of the Book of the Covenant, which had been found in the temple of the LORD. ³ The king stood by the pillar and renewed the covenant in the presence of the LORD—to follow the LORD and keep his commands, statutes and decrees with all his heart and all his soul, thus confirming the words of the covenant written in this book. Then all the people pledged themselves to the covenant.

⁴ The king ordered Hilkiah the high priest, the priests next in rank and the doorkeepers to remove from the temple of the Lord all the articles made for Baal and Asherah and all the starry hosts. He burned them outside Jerusalem in the fields of the Kidron Valley and took the ashes to Bethel. ⁵ He did away with the idolatrous priests appointed by the kings of Judah to burn incense on the high places of the towns of Judah and on those around Jerusalem—those who burned incense to Baal, to the sun and moon, to the constellations and to all the starry hosts. ⁶ He took the Asherah pole from the temple of the Lord to the Kidron Valley outside Jerusalem and burned it there. He ground it to powder and scattered the dust over the graves of the common people.

⁷ He also tore down the quarters of the male shrine prostitutes that were in the temple of the Lord, the quarters where women did weaving for Asherah.

⁸ Josiah brought all the priests from the towns of Judah and desecrated the high places, from Geba to Beersheba, where the priests had burned incense. He broke down the gateway at the entrance of the Gate of Joshua, the city governor, which was on the left of the city gate. ⁹ Although the priests of the high places did not serve at the altar of the Lord in Jerusalem, they ate unleavened bread with their fellow priests.

¹⁰ He desecrated Topheth, which was in the Valley of Ben Hinnom, so no one could use it to sacrifice their son or daughter in the fire to Molek. ¹¹ He removed from the entrance to the temple of the Lord the horses that the kings of Judah had dedicated to the sun. They were in the court near the room of an official named Nathan-Melek. Josiah then burned the chariots dedicated to the sun.

¹² He pulled down the altars the kings of Judah had erected on the roof near the upper room of Ahaz, and the altars Manasseh had built in the two courts of the temple of the Lord. He removed them from there, smashed them to pieces and threw the rubble into the Kidron Valley. ¹³ The king also desecrated the high places that were east of Jerusalem on the south of the Hill of Corruption—the ones Solomon king of Israel had built for Ashtoreth the vile goddess of the Sidonians, for Chemosh the vile god of Moab, and for Molek the detestable god of the people of Ammon. ¹⁴ Josiah smashed the sacred stones and cut down the Asherah poles and covered the sites with human bones.

¹⁵ Even the altar at Bethel, the high place made by Jeroboam son of Nebat, who had caused Israel to sin—even that altar and high place he demolished. He burned the high place and ground it to powder, and burned the Asherah pole also. ¹⁶ Then Josiah looked around, and when he saw the tombs that were there on the hillside, he had the bones removed from them and burned on the altar to defile it, in accordance with the word of the LORD proclaimed by the man of God who foretold these things. . . .

²⁴ Furthermore, Josiah got rid of the mediums and spiritists, the household gods, the idols and all the other detestable things seen in Judah and Jerusalem. This he did to fulfill the requirements of the law written in the book that Hilkiah the priest had discovered in the temple of the LORD. ²⁵ Neither before nor after Josiah was there a king like him who turned to the LORD as he did—with all his heart and with all his soul and with all his strength, in accordance with all the Law of Moses.

Study Questions

1. Why do you think Josiah read the Book of the Covenant to the people personally rather than asking a priest to do it?

   _____

   _____

   _____

   _____

2. The worship of other gods was a continual problem in Israel and Judah in the time of the kings, going all the way back to Solomon. What did Josiah do to try to stop this detestable practice? List as many actions as you can find. Why was he so thorough?

   _____

   _____

   _____

   _____

3. King David has been called a man after God's own heart, and King Solomon has been called the wisest man who ever lived, yet it was said of Josiah, "Neither before nor after Josiah was there a king like him who turned to the

Lᴏʀᴅ as he did—with all his heart and with all his soul and with all his strength, in accordance with all the Law of Moses." What is the significance of that statement? And what does it tell you God values in leaders?

_____

_____

_____

_____

2 Jesus' Example Stands for All Time

John 13:1–17, 34–35

¹ It was just before the Passover Festival. Jesus knew that the hour had come for him to leave this world and go to the Father. Having loved his own who were in the world, he loved them to the end.

² The evening meal was in progress, and the devil had already prompted Judas, the son of Simon Iscariot, to betray Jesus. ³ Jesus knew that the Father had put all things under his power, and that he had come from God and was returning to God; ⁴ so he got up from the meal, took off his outer clothing, and wrapped a towel around his waist. ⁵ After that, he poured water into a basin and began to wash his disciples' feet, drying them with the towel that was wrapped around him.

⁶ He came to Simon Peter, who said to him, "Lord, are you going to wash my feet?"

⁷ Jesus replied, "You do not realize now what I am doing, but later you will understand."

⁸ "No," said Peter, "you shall never wash my feet."

Jesus answered, "Unless I wash you, you have no part with me."

⁹ "Then, Lord," Simon Peter replied, "not just my feet but my hands and my head as well!"

¹⁰ Jesus answered, "Those who have had a bath need only to wash their feet; their whole body is clean. And you are clean, though not every one of you." ¹¹ For he knew who was going to betray him, and that was why he said not every one was clean.

¹² When he had finished washing their feet, he put on his clothes and returned to his place. "Do you understand what I have done for you?" he asked them. ¹³ *"You call me 'Teacher' and 'Lord,' and rightly so, for that is what I am. ¹⁴ Now that I, your Lord and Teacher, have washed your feet, you also should wash one another's feet. ¹⁵ I have set you an example that you should do as I have done for you. ¹⁶ Very truly I tell you, no servant is greater than his master, nor is a messenger greater than the one who sent him. ¹⁷ Now that you know these things, you will be blessed if you do them. . . .*

³⁴ "A new command I give you: Love one another. As I have loved you, so you must love one another. ³⁵ By this everyone will know that you are my disciples, if you love one another."

Study Questions

1. How much time do you think it took Jesus to perform this act of service where he undressed, washed the feet of twelve people, and got dressed again? Why did he go to all that trouble?

2. What do you think the disciples did and thought while Jesus was performing this subservient task? What lasting impression might they have come away with?

3. How did Peter respond to Jesus' intention to wash his feet? What does Jesus' response to Peter communicate about what is and what isn't a leader's responsibility while serving his people?

3 The Higher the Leader, the More Important the Example

1 Corinthians 4:1–4, 9, 11–17

¹ This, then, is how you ought to regard us: as servants of Christ and as those entrusted with the mysteries God has revealed. ² Now it is required that those who have been given a trust must prove faithful. ³ I care very little if I am judged by you or by any human court; indeed, I do not even judge myself. ⁴ My conscience is clear, but that does not make me innocent. It is the Lord who judges me. . . .

⁹ For it seems to me that God has put us apostles on display at the end of the procession, like those condemned to die in the arena. We have been made a spectacle to the whole universe, to angels as well as to human beings. . . .

¹¹ To this very hour we go hungry and thirsty, we are in rags, we are brutally treated, we are homeless. ¹² We work hard with our own hands. When we are cursed, we bless; when we are persecuted, we endure it; ¹³ when we are slandered, we answer kindly. We have become the scum of the earth, the garbage of the world—right up to this moment.

¹⁴ I am writing this not to shame you but to warn you as my dear children. ¹⁵ Even if you had ten thousand guardians in Christ, you do not have many fathers, for in Christ Jesus I became your father through the gospel. ¹⁶ Therefore I urge you to imitate me. ¹⁷ For this reason I have sent to you Timothy, my son whom I love, who is faithful in the Lord. He will remind you of my way of life in Christ Jesus, which agrees with what I teach everywhere in every church.

Study Questions

1. Paul writes about being given a trust by God. In what way is leadership of any kind a trust?

   _____

   _____

   _____

   _____

   _____

2. Why does Paul make a point of saying he doesn't care if others judge him and that he doesn't even judge himself? How does that idea relate to setting an example for others?

_____

_____

_____

_____

3. What are the challenges of being an example to others from a distance? How did Paul address these challenges?

_____

_____

_____

_____

4. In 1 Corinthians 12:28, Paul suggests that apostles are placed first in church leadership. In this passage he says that apostles have been put on display for others to see as an example. What truth does that suggest about the example that must be set by leaders with much responsibility?

_____

_____

_____

_____

LEADERSHIP INSIGHT AND REFLECTION

The three people highlighted in these passages are extraordinary leaders who set a high bar in leadership. However, you should not assume that setting the example was easy for them. What challenges do you think each of them may have faced in living out the Law of the Picture?

_____

_____

_____

_____

What challenges do you face in living the Law of the Picture and setting a positive example for the people you lead?

_____

_____

_____

_____

_____

_____

_____

TAKING ACTION

What thinking, attitudes, behaviors, and habits do you need to change to become a better example for the people you lead?

_____

_____

_____

_____

_____

_____

_____

_____

Make a list of the changes you need to make. For each item, set a starting date as well as a date by which you hope to complete the change.

Change	Start	Finish

Group Discussion Questions

1. What is your reaction to all the pagan practices Josiah was putting an end to among the Israelites—the worship of idols, heavens, and false gods; housing of prostitutes in the temple; and sacrifice of children? How do you think Josiah reacted emotionally and spiritually? What was his mindset? How do you think it impacted the way he led?

2. What do you think Jesus' mindset was as he washed the disciples' feet? What was his attitude? Explain.

3. How can leaders effectively communicate that they want the people they lead to emulate the example they are setting? How can they help people make that connection?

4. Paul's letter to the Corinthians encouraged them to follow his example. Do you think they would have gotten off track if he had been able to remain in Corinth? Explain your answer.

5. What is currently your greatest challenge in setting an example for others and why?

6. What was your greatest takeaway from this lesson?

7. In what way is God desiring you to change to become a better picture of leadership to others? How will you make that change?

LESSON 14

THE LAW OF BUY-IN

People Buy into the Leader, Then the Vision

DEFINITION OF THE LAW

Every leader would love to have a "dream team"—a unified group of followers who are passionate about the leader's vision and deeply committed to making it a reality. Of course, the size and significance of that vision is important. Followers need to believe in their cause. But wise leaders know that something else must always come first. People buy into the leader, *then* the vision. Not the other way around. That's the Law of Buy-In.

Many leaders have this backwards. They focus on coming up with and communicating an amazing vision. They believe that if the cause is good enough, people will automatically buy into it and follow. But that's not how it works. People don't at first follow worthy causes. They follow worthy leaders who promote causes they can believe in. The leader finds the dream and then the people. The people find the leader, and then the dream.

Even when people are passionate about a vision, if they don't buy into the leader, they aren't able to follow wholeheartedly. They won't give their all, and sometimes that means the vision can't be achieved. That's one reason why professional sports teams change coaches so often. The vision for all teams is the same, and every player already embraces it: everyone wants to win a championship. But if the players don't believe in their coach, they may find it impossible to have a winning season. When that happens, the owners don't change the goal or fire all of the players. They fire the coach and hire someone that they hope the players will buy into. After all, the talent level of most professional coaches is similar. The effectiveness of their systems doesn't differ much. What often varies is their leadership and their level of credibility with players.

When people believe in their leader and the vision, they will follow their leader no matter how bad conditions get or how much the odds are stacked against them. That's why the Indian people in Gandhi's day joined him in refusing to fight back even as soldiers mowed them down. That's what inspired the U.S. space program to fulfill John F. Kennedy's vision and put a man on the moon. That's the reason people continued to have hope and keep alive the dream of Martin Luther King Jr., even after he was gunned down. That's what continues to inspire followers to keep running the race, even when they feel they've hit the wall and given everything they've got.

To harness the Law of Buy-In, you need to focus first on becoming someone people would want to follow. It's all about developing trust. Once others are convinced of your credibility, they're willing to consider your cause. Credibility plus cause leads to commitment.

Once people respect and trust you, they'll follow you—and your vision—without reservation. And the more they respect you, the bigger the vision they'll embrace.

CASE STUDIES

Read these case studies from the Bible and answer the study questions that follow.

① A Test of Leadership Buy-In

Judges 7:2–25

> [2] The LORD said to Gideon, "You have too many men. I cannot deliver Midian into their hands, or Israel would boast against me, 'My own strength has saved me.' [3] Now announce to the army, 'Anyone who trembles with fear may turn back and leave Mount Gilead.'" So twenty-two thousand men left, while ten thousand remained.

⁴ But the LORD said to Gideon, "There are still too many men. Take them down to the water, and I will thin them out for you there. If I say, 'This one shall go with you,' he shall go; but if I say, 'This one shall not go with you,' he shall not go."

⁵ So Gideon took the men down to the water. There the LORD told him, "Separate those who lap the water with their tongues as a dog laps from those who kneel down to drink." ⁶ Three hundred of them drank from cupped hands, lapping like dogs. All the rest got down on their knees to drink.

⁷ The LORD said to Gideon, "With the three hundred men that lapped I will save you and give the Midianites into your hands. Let all the others go home." ⁸ So Gideon sent the rest of the Israelites home but kept the three hundred, who took over the provisions and trumpets of the others.

Now the camp of Midian lay below him in the valley. ⁹ During that night the LORD said to Gideon, "Get up, go down against the camp, because I am going to give it into your hands. ¹⁰ If you are afraid to attack, go down to the camp with your servant Purah ¹¹ and listen to what they are saying. Afterward, you will be encouraged to attack the camp." So he and Purah his servant went down to the outposts of the camp. ¹² The Midianites, the Amalekites and all the other eastern peoples had settled in the valley, thick as locusts. Their camels could no more be counted than the sand on the seashore.

¹³ Gideon arrived just as a man was telling a friend his dream. "I had a dream," he was saying. "A round loaf of barley bread came tumbling into the Midianite camp. It struck the tent with such force that the tent overturned and collapsed."

¹⁴ His friend responded, "This can be nothing other than the sword of Gideon son of Joash, the Israelite. God has given the Midianites and the whole camp into his hands."

¹⁵ When Gideon heard the dream and its interpretation, he bowed down and worshiped. He returned to the camp of Israel and called out, "Get up! The LORD has given the Midianite camp into your hands." ¹⁶ Dividing the three hundred men into three companies, he placed trumpets and empty jars in the hands of all of them, with torches inside.

¹⁷ "Watch me," he told them. "Follow my lead. When I get to the edge of the camp, do exactly as I do. ¹⁸ When I and all who are with me blow our trumpets, then from all around the camp blow yours and shout, 'For the LORD and for Gideon.'"

¹⁹ *Gideon and the hundred men with him reached the edge of the camp at the beginning of the middle watch, just after they had changed the guard. They blew their trumpets and broke the jars that were in their hands.*
²⁰ *The three companies blew the trumpets and smashed the jars. Grasping the torches in their left hands and holding in their right hands the trumpets they were to blow, they shouted, "A sword for the Lord and for Gideon!"*
²¹ *While each man held his position around the camp, all the Midianites ran, crying out as they fled.*

²² *When the three hundred trumpets sounded, the Lord caused the men throughout the camp to turn on each other with their swords. The army fled to Beth Shittah toward Zererah as far as the border of Abel Meholah near Tabbath.* ²³ *Israelites from Naphtali, Asher and all Manasseh were called out, and they pursued the Midianites.* ²⁴ *Gideon sent messengers throughout the hill country of Ephraim, saying, "Come down against the Midianites and seize the waters of the Jordan ahead of them as far as Beth Barah."*

So all the men of Ephraim were called out and they seized the waters of the Jordan as far as Beth Barah. ²⁵ *They also captured two of the Midianite leaders, Oreb and Zeeb. They killed Oreb at the rock of Oreb, and Zeeb at the winepress of Zeeb. They pursued the Midianites and brought the heads of Oreb and Zeeb to Gideon, who was by the Jordan.*

Study Questions

1. Gideon obviously bought into God as his leader prior to the thinning of the Israelites who would go into battle. How difficult would it have been for you to keep buying into God and obeying him as he reduced your fighting force from thirty-two thousand to three hundred?

_____

_____

_____

_____

_____

_____

2. If there was resistance from the Israelites to Gideon's plan for fighting the huge army of Midianites, it's not recorded in the passage. If you were one of the three hundred, what would you have been thinking?

_____

_____

_____

_____

_____

3. What do you think would have happened if the three hundred had not followed Gideon's leadership?

_____

_____

_____

_____

_____

_____

_____

❷ Buying into a Bold Vision

Nehemiah 2:1–18

¹ In the month of Nisan in the twentieth year of King Artaxerxes, when wine was brought for him, I took the wine and gave it to the king. I had not been sad in his presence before, ² so the king asked me, "Why does your face look so sad when you are not ill? This can be nothing but sadness of heart."

I was very much afraid, ³ but I said to the king, "May the king live forever! Why should my face not look sad when the city where my ancestors are buried lies in ruins, and its gates have been destroyed by fire?"

⁴ The king said to me, "What is it you want?"

Then I prayed to the God of heaven, ⁵ and I answered the king, "If it pleases the king and if your servant has found favor in his sight, let him send me to the city in Judah where my ancestors are buried so that I can rebuild it."

6 Then the king, with the queen sitting beside him, asked me, "How long will your journey take, and when will you get back?" It pleased the king to send me; so I set a time.

7 I also said to him, "If it pleases the king, may I have letters to the governors of Trans-Euphrates, so that they will provide me safe-conduct until I arrive in Judah? 8 And may I have a letter to Asaph, keeper of the royal park, so he will give me timber to make beams for the gates of the citadel by the temple and for the city wall and for the residence I will occupy?" And because the gracious hand of my God was on me, the king granted my requests. 9 So I went to the governors of Trans-Euphrates and gave them the king's letters. The king had also sent army officers and cavalry with me.

10 When Sanballat the Horonite and Tobiah the Ammonite official heard about this, they were very much disturbed that someone had come to promote the welfare of the Israelites.

11 I went to Jerusalem, and after staying there three days 12 I set out during the night with a few others. I had not told anyone what my God had put in my heart to do for Jerusalem. There were no mounts with me except the one I was riding on.

13 By night I went out through the Valley Gate toward the Jackal Well and the Dung Gate, examining the walls of Jerusalem, which had been broken down, and its gates, which had been destroyed by fire. 14 Then I moved on toward the Fountain Gate and the King's Pool, but there was not enough room for my mount to get through; 15 so I went up the valley by night, examining the wall. Finally, I turned back and reentered through the Valley Gate. 16 The officials did not know where I had gone or what I was doing, because as yet I had said nothing to the Jews or the priests or nobles or officials or any others who would be doing the work.

17 Then I said to them, "You see the trouble we are in: Jerusalem lies in ruins, and its gates have been burned with fire. Come, let us rebuild the wall of Jerusalem, and we will no longer be in disgrace." 18 I also told them about the gracious hand of my God on me and what the king had said to me.

They replied, "Let us start rebuilding." So they began this good work.

Study Questions

1. How would you describe the relationship between King Artaxerxes and Nehemiah, his cupbearer? Who bought into whom? What evidence can you give to support your opinion?

   _____

   _____

   _____

   _____

   _____

   _____

2. How bold and risky was Nehemiah's vision to rebuild the walls of Jerusalem? Explain.

   _____

   _____

   _____

   _____

   _____

   _____

3. Sanballat and Tobiah were governors in the Trans-Euphrates region. What does their reaction say about their opinion of Nehemiah?

   _____

   _____

   _____

   _____

   _____

   _____

4. Why do you think the officials in Jerusalem agreed to start rebuilding the walls?

   _____

   _____

   _____

   _____

   _____

   _____

❸ Remaining Confident in Christ

Hebrews 3:1–15

¹ Therefore, holy brothers and sisters, who share in the heavenly calling, fix your thoughts on Jesus, whom we acknowledge as our apostle and high priest. ² He was faithful to the one who appointed him, just as Moses was faithful in all God's house. ³ Jesus has been found worthy of greater honor than Moses, just as the builder of a house has greater honor than the house itself. ⁴ For every house is built by someone, but God is the builder of everything. ⁵ "Moses was faithful as a servant in all God's house," bearing witness to what would be spoken by God in the future. ⁶ But Christ is faithful as the Son over God's house. And we are his house, if indeed we hold firmly to our confidence and the hope in which we glory.

⁷ So, as the Holy Spirit says:

> *"Today, if you hear his voice,*
> *⁸ do not harden your hearts*
> *as you did in the rebellion,*
> *during the time of testing in the wilderness,*
> *⁹ where your ancestors tested and tried me,*
> *though for forty years they saw what I did.*
> *¹⁰ That is why I was angry with that generation;*
> *I said, 'Their hearts are always going astray,*
> *and they have not known my ways.'*
> *¹¹ So I declared on oath in my anger,*
> *'They shall never enter my rest.'"*

¹² See to it, brothers and sisters, that none of you has a sinful, unbelieving heart that turns away from the living God. ¹³ But encourage one another daily, as long as it is called "Today," so that none of you may be hardened by sin's deceitfulness. ¹⁴ We have come to share in Christ, if indeed we hold our original conviction firmly to the very end. ¹⁵ As has just been said:

"Today, if you hear his voice,
do not harden your hearts
as you did in the rebellion."

Study Questions

1. The rebellion in the wilderness mentioned in this passage refers to the time when the children of Israel refused to go into the Promised Land. What does their refusal say about their buy-in to Moses and God as their leaders?

_____

_____

_____

_____

2. Why do you think the writer of Hebrews warns the brothers and sisters who share in the heavenly calling not to harden their hearts?

_____

_____

_____

_____

_____

3. Jesus Christ is the leader of every person who has put faith in him. What is the evidence of buying into him?

_____

_____

_____

_____

4. Where are you falling short in your buy-in and obedience to him as your leader?

_____

_____

_____

_____

LEADERSHIP INSIGHT AND REFLECTION

What are the roles of the mind and heart in leadership buy-in? What about faith?

_____
_____
_____
_____
_____
_____
_____
_____
_____
_____

Where do you need to grow as a follower?

_____
_____
_____
_____
_____
_____
_____
_____

Where do you need to grow as a leader so that you become worthy of followership?

_____
_____
_____
_____
_____
_____
_____
_____

TAKING ACTION

Think about your answer to the last two questions. Where do you most need to grow and change to become a better leader? In your followership of Christ? Or in your character as a leader? Explain.

_____

_____

_____

_____

_____

_____

_____

_____

_____

_____

What tangible step will you take immediately to resolve this issue?

_____

_____

_____

_____

_____

_____

_____

_____

_____

_____

GROUP DISCUSSION QUESTIONS

1. How do you think Gideon's followers felt going into battle with trumpets and torches instead of weapons? What would you have said to them as their leader to reassure them?

2. When the Midianites fled, Gideon sent messengers asking the Ephraimites to join the battle, and they responded immediately. Why do you think they did? And why did God allow more people to help at that time, where he wanted only three hundred people involved in the original assault?

3. Nehemiah is often credited with being one of the finest examples of leadership in the Bible. Why do you think that is?

4. Which do you usually find it easier to buy into: a powerful or charismatic leader who leads from a distance, or a leader you know personally who's closer to you in the organization's hierarchy? Why?

5. What is the greatest challenge you have to getting buy-in from the people you're leading?

6. What do you typically do to gain that buy-in? How well does it work?

7. What changes in your leadership do you believe you need to make as a result of this lesson? How do you intend to change and when will you take action?

LESSON 15

THE LAW OF VICTORY

Leaders Find a Way for the Team to Win

DEFINITION OF THE LAW

Winston Churchill. Franklin D. Roosevelt. Nelson Mandela. Famous world leaders who snatched victory from the jaws of defeat. Churchill led the British to hold off a Nazi invasion. Roosevelt led Americans through the Great Depression. And Mandela led South Africans to rise up and dismantle the injustice of apartheid. What did they all have in common, besides seemingly insurmountable challenges? They found a way for their people to win.

Have you ever thought about what separates the leaders who achieve victory from those who suffer defeat? What does it take to make a team a winner? Every leadership situation is different, and every crisis has its own challenges. But leaders who win, especially those who overcome impossible odds, have one thing in common: they share a complete unwillingness to accept defeat. The alternative to winning is totally unacceptable to them. They have no Plan B. As a result, they refuse to stop fighting until they achieve victory.

This commitment to winning is deep inside these kinds of leaders. They're known for it based on how they handled challenges in the past. They keep demonstrating it regardless of circumstances. Crisis always brings out the best—and the worst—in people. Problems magnify internal character. When the pressure is intense, and the stakes are high, great leaders rise up and find a way for the team to win. That's the Law of Victory.

Leaders who win possess unlimited belief, commitment, resourcefulness, and perseverance. These are mindsets that any leader can develop. You can grow in them and increase your likelihood of winning. And as you demonstrate these traits, you will inspire them in your people.

Winning leaders continually believe and inspire belief. Choose daily to be completely confident—not only in your team's ability to win but also in your reason for winning. Keep your eyes on the prize and strategize how you'll get there. Then demonstrate your belief through everything you do and say. This will draw people to you and encourage them to believe as well.

It's crucial to commit completely and encourage that commitment in your team. Winning leaders do what it takes to win. They are willing to put everything on the line—their reputation, resources, freedom, even their lives—for the cause. And they go first. You must lead the charge, regardless of obstacles in your way. When you are willing to risk everything in pursuit of victory, you'll inspire your team to join in the battle.

Winning leaders maximize all available resources and expect their people to do likewise. Look at problems creatively, believing there is always a solution. Use everything you have at hand. When you don't have the right people or resources, go get them. No matter how difficult it is to recruit the right person or build a solution, you have to keep at it until you win. As you model creative problem-solving, your people will follow your lead.

Finally, persevere and require perseverance from your team. This is the most important quality of leaders who achieve victory. After believing, committing, and problem-solving, they just keep going. They continue to push until they reach the goal. And they exhort their followers, as Churchill famously did, to "never, never, never give up." That is the Law of Victory in action.

CASE STUDIES

Read these case studies from the Bible and answer the study questions that follow.

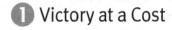 **Victory at a Cost**

Judges 16:1, 15–31

¹ One day Samson went to Gaza, where he saw a prostitute [named Delilah]. He went in to spend the night with her. . . .

¹⁵ Then she said to him, "How can you say, 'I love you,' when you won't confide in me? This is the third time you have made a fool of me and haven't told me the secret of your great strength." ¹⁶ With such nagging she prodded him day after day until he was sick to death of it.

¹⁷ So he told her everything. "No razor has ever been used on my head," he said, "because I have been a Nazirite dedicated to God from my mother's womb. If my head were shaved, my strength would leave me, and I would become as weak as any other man."

¹⁸ When Delilah saw that he had told her everything, she sent word to the rulers of the Philistines, "Come back once more; he has told me everything." So the rulers of the Philistines returned with the silver in their hands. ¹⁹ After putting him to sleep on her lap, she called for someone to shave off the seven braids of his hair, and so began to subdue him. And his strength left him.

²⁰ Then she called, "Samson, the Philistines are upon you!"

He awoke from his sleep and thought, "I'll go out as before and shake myself free." But he did not know that the Lᴏʀᴅ had left him.

²¹ Then the Philistines seized [Samson], gouged out his eyes and took him down to Gaza. Binding him with bronze shackles, they set him to grinding grain in the prison. ²² But the hair on his head began to grow again after it had been shaved.

²³ Now the rulers of the Philistines assembled to offer a great sacrifice to Dagon their god and to celebrate, saying, "Our god has delivered Samson, our enemy, into our hands."

²⁴ When the people saw him, they praised their god, saying,

"Our god has delivered our enemy
    into our hands,
the one who laid waste our land
    and multiplied our slain."

²⁵ While they were in high spirits, they shouted, "Bring out Samson to entertain us." So they called Samson out of the prison, and he performed for them.

When they stood him among the pillars, ²⁶ Samson said to the servant who held his hand, "Put me where I can feel the pillars that support the temple, so that I may lean against them." ²⁷ Now the temple was crowded with men and *women; all the rulers of the Philistines were there, and on the roof were about three thousand men and women watching Samson perform. [28] Then Samson prayed to the LORD, "Sovereign LORD, remember me. Please, God, strengthen me just once more, and let me with one blow get revenge on the Philistines for my two eyes." [29] Then Samson reached toward the two central pillars on which the temple stood. Bracing himself against them, his right hand on the one and his left hand on the other, [30] Samson said, "Let me die with the Philistines!" Then he pushed with all his might, and down came the temple on the rulers and all the people in it. Thus he killed many more when he died than while he lived.*

[31] Then his brothers and his father's whole family went down to get him. They brought him back and buried him between Zorah and Eshtaol in the tomb of Manoah his father. He had led Israel twenty years.

Study Questions

1. Even before Samson was born, God selected him to lead the Israelites against their oppressors, the Philistines. Yet, he risked not fulfilling his calling. Why?

_____

_____

_____

_____

2. If Samson had been obedient to God, how might his path been different?

_____

_____

_____

_____

3. Ultimately, Samson won a victory for Israel, but it cost him his life. What lessons does this teach about the sovereignty of God, the consequences of sin, and the Law of Victory?

_____

_____

_____

_____

② Jonathan Initiates the Battle

1 Samuel 14:1–23

¹One day Jonathan son of Saul said to his young armor-bearer, "Come, let's go over to the Philistine outpost on the other side." But he did not tell his father.

² Saul was staying on the outskirts of Gibeah under a pomegranate tree in Migron. With him were about six hundred men, ³among whom was Ahijah, who was wearing an ephod. He was a son of Ichabod's brother Ahitub son of Phinehas, the son of Eli, the Lord's priest in Shiloh. No one was aware that Jonathan had left.

⁴ On each side of the pass that Jonathan intended to cross to reach the Philistine outpost was a cliff; one was called Bozez and the other Seneh. ⁵ One cliff stood to the north toward Mikmash, the other to the south toward Geba.

⁶ Jonathan said to his young armor-bearer, "Come, let's go over to the outpost of those uncircumcised men. Perhaps the Lord will act in our behalf. Nothing can hinder the Lord from saving, whether by many or by few."

⁷ "Do all that you have in mind," his armor-bearer said. "Go ahead; I am with you heart and soul."

⁸ Jonathan said, "Come on, then; we will cross over toward them and let them see us. ⁹ If they say to us, 'Wait there until we come to you,' we will stay where we are and not go up to them. ¹⁰ But if they say, 'Come up to us,' we will climb up, because that will be our sign that the Lord has given them into our hands."

¹¹ So both of them showed themselves to the Philistine outpost. "Look!" said the Philistines. "The Hebrews are crawling out of the holes they were hiding in." ¹² The men of the outpost shouted to Jonathan and his armor-bearer, "Come up to us and we'll teach you a lesson."

So Jonathan said to his armor-bearer, "Climb up after me; the Lord has given them into the hand of Israel."

¹³ Jonathan climbed up, using his hands and feet, with his armor-bearer right behind him. The Philistines fell before Jonathan, and his armor-bearer followed and killed behind him. ¹⁴ In that first attack Jonathan and his armor-bearer killed some twenty men in an area of about half an acre.

15 Then panic struck the whole army—those in the camp and field, and those in the outposts and raiding parties—and the ground shook. It was a panic sent by God.

16 Saul's lookouts at Gibeah in Benjamin saw the army melting away in all directions. 17 Then Saul said to the men who were with him, "Muster the forces and see who has left us." When they did, it was Jonathan and his armor-bearer who were not there.

18 Saul said to Ahijah, "Bring the ark of God." (At that time it was with the Israelites.) 19 While Saul was talking to the priest, the tumult in the Philistine camp increased more and more. So Saul said to the priest, "Withdraw your hand."

20 Then Saul and all his men assembled and went to the battle. They found the Philistines in total confusion, striking each other with their swords. 21 Those Hebrews who had previously been with the Philistines and had gone up with them to their camp went over to the Israelites who were with Saul and Jonathan. 22 When all the Israelites who had hidden in the hill country of Ephraim heard that the Philistines were on the run, they joined the battle in hot pursuit. 23 So on that day the LORD saved Israel, and the battle moved on beyond Beth Aven.

Study Questions

1. Why do you think Jonathan decided to go on the offensive against the Philistines?

   _____

   _____

   _____

   _____

2. How did Jonathan and his armor-bearer work together to be successful?

   _____

   _____

   _____

   _____

   _____

3. The writer attributes the ultimate victory to God. What were the roles of Jonathan and King Saul? What do you believe would have happened if Jonathan had not initiated the battle?

_____

_____

_____

_____

_____

_____

③ Finding a Way

Mark 2:1–12

¹ A few days later, when Jesus again entered Capernaum, the people heard that he had come home. ² They gathered in such large numbers that there was no room left, not even outside the door, and he preached the word to them. ³ Some men came, bringing to him a paralyzed man, carried by four of them. ⁴ Since they could not get him to Jesus because of the crowd, they made an opening in the roof above Jesus by digging through it and then lowered the mat the man was lying on. ⁵ When Jesus saw their faith, he said to the paralyzed man, "Son, your sins are forgiven."

⁶ Now some teachers of the law were sitting there, thinking to themselves, ⁷ "Why does this fellow talk like that? He's blaspheming! Who can forgive sins but God alone?"

⁸ Immediately Jesus knew in his spirit that this was what they were thinking in their hearts, and he said to them, "Why are you thinking these things? ⁹ Which is easier: to say to this paralyzed man, 'Your sins are forgiven,' or to say, 'Get up, take your mat and walk'? ¹⁰ But I want you to know that the Son of Man has authority on earth to forgive sins." So he said to the man, ¹¹ "I tell you, get up, take your mat and go home." ¹² He got up, took his mat and walked out in full view of them all. This amazed everyone and they praised God, saying, "We have never seen anything like this!"

Study Questions

1. How did the companions of the paralyzed man practice the Law of Victory? Why do you think they took it as far as they did?

_____

_____

_____

_____

2. Do you believe one of the companions was the ringleader? Explain.

_____

_____

_____

_____

3. How did Jesus practice the Law of Victory? Why do you think he took things as far as he did?

_____

_____

_____

_____

LEADERSHIP INSIGHT AND REFLECTION

Which person do you identify with in the passages?

- Samson—you've made mistakes and it's costing you
- Jonathan—you're the one who initiates victories
- The armor-bearer—you assist a leader who wins battles
- The paralyzed man—you benefit from others' victories
- The paralyzed man's companions—you are part of a team who wins
- Jesus—you win victories and others are amazed by it

Explain your answer.

_____

_____

_____

_____

_____

For you to become a leader who finds ways for your team to win, would you need to change your attitude, thinking, habits, or methods? How would you need to change?

_____

_____

_____

_____

TAKING ACTION

What will you *stop doing* to practice the Law of Victory as a leader?

_____

_____

_____

_____

_____

What will you start doing to practice the Law of Victory as a leader?

_____

_____

_____

_____

When will you do it?   Date:_____

GROUP DISCUSSION QUESTIONS

1. Would you consider Samson's destruction of the temple and death of the Philistines a victory, a defeat, or something in between?

2. Why do you think Jonathan didn't tell his father Saul that he was going out to attack the Philistines?

3. Jonathan declared that if the Philistines called them to come up to where they were, then God had put the Philistines into Israel's hands. As a leader, what is your reaction to something like that? And how do you translate it into your everyday leadership?

4. Do you think the companions *knew* that taking the paralyzed man to Jesus would lead to a victory, or do you think they just hoped for the best?

5. As a leader, how do you define whether something is a victory?

6. What was your greatest takeaway about leadership in this lesson?

7. How do you believe God is asking you to change your approach to leadership as a result of this lesson? When and how will you do it?

LESSON 16

THE LAW OF THE BIG MO

Momentum Is a Leader's Best Friend

DEFINITION OF THE LAW

If you've got all the passion, tools, and people you need to fulfill a great vision, yet you can't seem to get your organization moving and going in the right direction, you're dead in the water as a leader. If you can't get things going, you will not succeed. What do you need in such circumstances? You need to look to the Law of the Big Mo and harness the power of the leader's best friend: momentum.

When you have no momentum, even the simplest tasks seem impossible. Small problems look like insurmountable obstacles. An organization with no momentum is like a train at a dead stop. It's hard to get going, and even small wooden blocks on the track can keep it from going anywhere. In contrast, when you have momentum on your side, the future looks bright and troubles seem inconsequential. An organization with momentum is like a train that's moving at 60 miles per hour. You could build a steel-reinforced concrete wall across the tracks, and the train would plow right through it.

Momentum is the great exaggerator. It's like a magnifying glass; it makes every situation look better than it really is. When the team is on a winning streak, players feel like they can do no wrong. They don't focus on injuries or errors; they just look for ways to win. Momentum also exaggerates the leader's contribution to team success. People start thinking you're a genius. They look past your shortcomings and forget about your mistakes. The more you win, the more people expect you to keep winning. But momentum is not just about perception. It also improves performance. As the team maintains momentum, its members keep performing better than they ever thought possible. They break records and exceed expectations.

Given enough momentum, even the biggest disruption is possible. It's a powerful change agent. People like to associate with winners, and they tend to get on a winning bandwagon. Followers trust leaders with a proven track record. They more readily accept even huge changes from people who have led them to victory before.

How is momentum created? It requires someone who has vision, can assemble a good team, and motivates others. In other words, it is the leader's responsibility to both initiate momentum and keep it going. If you as the leader are waiting for someone else to motivate you or to develop momentum in the organization, then everyone is in trouble. It starts inside of you, with your vision, passion, and enthusiasm.

To build momentum, you need to enthusiastically pursue the vision, doing all that you can to achieve small wins. Those successes will get the ball rolling, and momentum will begin to build. Continue to model enthusiasm to your people day in and day out, attract like-minded people to your team, and motivate them to achieve, and momentum will continue. And if you're wise, you'll always value it for what it is: the leader's best friend. Once you have it, you can do almost anything. That's the power of the Big Mo.

CASE STUDIES

Read these case studies from the Bible and answer the study questions that follow.

 Early Victories

Deuteronomy 2:24–37

[24] *"Set out now and cross the Arnon Gorge. See, I have given into your hand Sihon the Amorite, king of Heshbon, and his country. Begin to take possession*

of it and engage him in battle. ²⁵ *This very day I will begin to put the terror and fear of you on all the nations under heaven. They will hear reports of you and will tremble and be in anguish because of you."*

²⁶ *From the Desert of Kedemoth I sent messengers to Sihon king of Heshbon offering peace and saying,* ²⁷ *"Let us pass through your country. We will stay on the main road; we will not turn aside to the right or to the left.* ²⁸ *Sell us food to eat and water to drink for their price in silver. Only let us pass through on foot—* ²⁹ *as the descendants of Esau, who live in Seir, and the Moabites, who live in Ar, did for us—until we cross the Jordan into the land the Lord our God is giving us."* ³⁰ *But Sihon king of Heshbon refused to let us pass through. For the Lord your God had made his spirit stubborn and his heart obstinate in order to give him into your hands, as he has now done.*

³¹ *The Lord said to me, "See, I have begun to deliver Sihon and his country over to you. Now begin to conquer and possess his land."*

³² *When Sihon and all his army came out to meet us in battle at Jahaz,* ³³ *the Lord our God delivered him over to us and we struck him down, together with his sons and his whole army.* ³⁴ *At that time we took all his towns and completely destroyed them—men, women and children. We left no survivors.* ³⁵ *But the livestock and the plunder from the towns we had captured we carried off for ourselves.* ³⁶ *From Aroer on the rim of the Arnon Gorge, and from the town in the gorge, even as far as Gilead, not one town was too strong for us. The Lord our God gave us all of them.* ³⁷ *But in accordance with the command of the Lord our God, you did not encroach on any of the land of the Ammonites, neither the land along the course of the Jabbok nor that around the towns in the hills.*

Deuteronomy 3:1–11

¹ *Next we turned and went up along the road toward Bashan, and Og king of Bashan with his whole army marched out to meet us in battle at Edrei.* ² *The Lord said to me, "Do not be afraid of him, for I have delivered him into your hands, along with his whole army and his land. Do to him what you did to Sihon king of the Amorites, who reigned in Heshbon."*

³ *So the Lord our God also gave into our hands Og king of Bashan and all his army. We struck them down, leaving no survivors.* ⁴ *At that time we took all*

his cities. There was not one of the sixty cities that we did not take from them— the whole region of Argob, Og's kingdom in Bashan. ⁵ All these cities were fortified with high walls and with gates and bars, and there were also a great many unwalled villages. ⁶ We completely destroyed them, as we had done with Sihon king of Heshbon, destroying every city—men, women and children. ⁷ But all the livestock and the plunder from their cities we carried off for ourselves.

⁸ So at that time we took from these two kings of the Amorites the territory east of the Jordan, from the Arnon Gorge as far as Mount Hermon. ⁹ (Hermon is called Sirion by the Sidonians; the Amorites call it Senir.) ¹⁰ We took all the towns on the plateau, and all Gilead, and all Bashan as far as Salekah and Edrei, towns of Og's kingdom in Bashan. ¹¹ (Og king of Bashan was the last of the Rephaites. His bed was decorated with iron and was more than nine cubits long and four cubits wide. It is still in Rabbah of the Ammonites.)

Study Questions

1. The book of Deuteronomy begins with Moses recounting the events of the Israelites' disobedience: their refusal to obey God's original command to go into the Promised Land, the battle against the Amorites they lost when they attempted it without God's blessing, and their wandering in the desert for forty years. Why do you think Moses wrote about this history before writing about their victories?

   _____

   _____

   _____

   _____

2. Knowing that the Israelites had lost a battle with the Amorites before their forty years in the wilderness, what progression of momentum do you see in the defeat of the Amorite king Sihon of Heshbon and king Og of Bashan?

   _____

   _____

   _____

   _____

3. The victories over these two kings and their territories occurred east of the Jordan River, before the Israelites crossed into the Promised Land. Why do you think God gave them victories there instead of prompting the kings to let them have safe passage as they originally requested? What leadership lesson does that teach you?

_____

_____

_____

_____

_____

_____

_____

_____

_____

2 A Missed Opportunity for Momentum

2 Kings 13:14–19

14 Now Elisha had been suffering from the illness from which he died. Jehoash king of Israel went down to see him and wept over him. "My father! My father!" he cried. "The chariots and horsemen of Israel!"

15 Elisha said, "Get a bow and some arrows," and he did so. 16 "Take the bow in your hands," he said to the king of Israel. When he had taken it, Elisha put his hands on the king's hands.

17 "Open the east window," he said, and he opened it. "Shoot!" Elisha said, and he shot. "The LORD's arrow of victory, the arrow of victory over Aram!" Elisha declared. "You will completely destroy the Arameans at Aphek."

18 Then he said, "Take the arrows," and the king took them. Elisha told him, "Strike the ground." He struck it three times and stopped. 19 The man of God was angry with him and said, "You should have struck the ground five or six times; then you would have defeated Aram and completely destroyed it. But now you will defeat it only three times."

Study Questions

1. Why do you think Elisha asked Jehoash to first shoot the arrow through the window before asking him to strike the ground with arrows?

   _____

   _____

   _____

   _____

2. The Israelites' conflicts with Aram traced all the way back to the time of the Judges. And they continued long after Jehoash was no longer king. Knowing that, what is the significance of Elisha's statement that if the king had stuck the ground many more times, Aram would have been completely destroyed? Explain.

   _____

   _____

   _____

   _____

3. What is the connection between the leadership of Jehoash and the success of Israel? Describe it. What words would you use to characterize Jehoash's leadership?

   _____

   _____

   _____

   _____

   _____

③ The Gospel Catches Fire

Acts 2:29–47

29 [Addressing the crowd, Peter said,] "Fellow Israelites, I can tell you confidently that the patriarch David died and was buried, and his tomb is here to this day. 30 But he was a prophet and knew that God had promised him on oath that he would place one of his descendants on his throne. 31 Seeing what was to come, he spoke of the resurrection of the Messiah, that he was not abandoned to the realm of the dead, nor did his body see decay. 32 God has raised this Jesus to life, and we are all witnesses of it. 33 Exalted to the right hand of God, he has received from the Father the promised Holy Spirit and has poured out what you now see and hear. 34 For David did not ascend to heaven, and yet he said,

> "'The Lord said to my Lord:
>   "Sit at my right hand
> 35 until I make your enemies
>   a footstool for your feet.'"

36 "Therefore let all Israel be assured of this: God has made this Jesus, whom you crucified, both Lord and Messiah."

37 When the people heard this, they were cut to the heart and said to Peter and the other apostles, "Brothers, what shall we do?"

38 Peter replied, "Repent and be baptized, every one of you, in the name of Jesus Christ for the forgiveness of your sins. And you will receive the gift of the Holy Spirit. 39 The promise is for you and your children and for all who are far off—for all whom the Lord our God will call."

40 With many other words he warned them; and he pleaded with them, "Save yourselves from this corrupt generation." 41 Those who accepted his message were baptized, and about three thousand were added to their number that day.

42 They devoted themselves to the apostles' teaching and to fellowship, to the breaking of bread and to prayer. 43 Everyone was filled with awe at the many wonders and signs performed by the apostles. 44 All the believers were together and had everything in common. 45 They sold property and possessions to give to anyone who had need. 46 Every day they continued to meet together in the temple courts. They broke bread in their homes and ate together with glad and sincere hearts, 47 praising God and enjoying the favor of all the people. And the Lord added to their number daily those who were being saved.

Study Questions

1. Prior to this first sermon of Peter recorded in the passage, the people of Jerusalem were largely against Jesus and the disciples. What is the significance of so many people repenting, believing in Jesus, and being baptized?

_____

_____

_____

_____

_____

_____

2. Acts 4:4 says, "The number of men who believed grew to about five thousand" after Peter and John preached, and Acts 6:7 says, "So the word of God spread. The number of disciples in Jerusalem increased rapidly, and a large number of priests became obedient to the faith." Without diminishing the role of the Holy Spirit, who had been given to Peter and the disciples right before he spoke to the crowd, what was the role of Peter, John, and the other apostles as leaders during this early season of the church?

_____

_____

_____

_____

_____

_____

3. How did the occurrences in Jerusalem immediately after Jesus' death and resurrection impact the spread of the faith?

_____

_____

_____

_____

_____

_____

Leadership Insight and Reflection

Based on the passages you read, what are the roles and responsibilities of God, leaders, and followers when it comes to the Law of the Big Mo?

_____

_____

_____

_____

_____

Based on your reading, what are the greatest enemies of momentum for a leader? Name as many as you can, both internal and external.

_____

_____

_____

_____

_____

Taking Action

What do you ordinarily do to prepare yourself for your role as a follower and as a leader when it comes to creating and sustaining momentum?

_____

_____

_____

_____

What do you need to do differently as a leader to make yourself a better candidate for generating momentum and having your team benefit from its power? How will you change and when will you initiate it?

_____

_____

_____

_____

Group Discussion Questions

1. Why do you think Moses suggested a peace agreement with Sihon king of Heshbon and offered to pay him for safe passage through his territory?

2. What was the benefit to the Israelites of Sihon attacking them?

3. If you had been King Jehoash and Elisha had asked you to strike the ground, what would you have done? Would you have known what Elisha was up to? How many times would you have struck the ground?

4. Jesus renamed Simon "Peter" because he said the disciple was the rock upon which he would build his church (Matthew 16:18). But Peter also denied Jesus (Luke 22:57). If you were one of the other disciples, would you have expected Peter to preach so boldly and effectively that three thousand people came to Christ in one day? Explain your answer.

5. What other examples from the Bible can you recall that illustrate the Law of the Big Mo, either positively or negatively?

6. What was your greatest takeaway about the Law of the Big Mo from this lesson? How does it relate to your leadership situation?

7. What changes in your leadership do you believe God is asking you to make to harness momentum for your team or organization? How will you change and when will you start?

LESSON 17

THE LAW OF PRIORITIES

Leaders Understand that Activity Is Not Necessarily Accomplishment

DEFINITION OF THE LAW

In today's fast-paced world, everyone seems to celebrate busyness. They see it as a sign of success and achievement. And the busier you are, the more you must be accomplishing, right? Wrong. Busyness does not equal productivity. Filling your schedule with activity is not necessarily accomplishment. The key is filling your time with the right activity. That's the Law of Priorities.

All leaders need to prioritize. There are just not enough hours in the day to do everything that we need or want done. It's essential to choose and order tasks wisely. This requires ongoing intentional effort. We need to regularly think ahead, determine what's important, discern what's next, and see how everything relates to the overall vision. Then put only the right tasks on our own to-do list, in the right order. That takes a lot of time and energy. And it won't happen unless we make it happen.

If you don't give time to the process of prioritizing, your task list will master you instead of the other way around. You'll be driven by the urgent, without ever evaluating whether what you're doing is actually important. You will be busy but not productive.

Begin by making a list of every value or commitment that you consider important. This could include everything from health objectives and worthy causes to work goals and relationships. Determine what really matters to you. Does everything line up with how you're currently spending your time? If you value exercise, is it on your calendar? If you consider family very important, how much time did you spend with them in the last week? By planning your time based on your actual priorities, your daily activities will result in accomplishment, not just busyness.

For years, I've prioritized my calendar and to-do list with the three Rs. No, not the ones you learned in school. My three Rs are requirement, return, and reward. Create a task list by answering these three questions, in order:

First, what is required? Whether to meet a boss's expectations or to fulfill your role as a parent, friend, or spouse, you know that some tasks are nonnegotiable and must be high on your priority list. If you're not sure if they are actual requirements, ask, "What must I do that no one else can or should do for me?" If it's not a must-do, it shouldn't go on your list. If it is necessary but not required of you personally, it should go on someone else's list. (In other words, delegate it.)

Second, what gives the greatest return? Where can your efforts make the most impact? Most likely in your areas of greatest strength. The priorities that make it into this next section of your list should be tasks that no one on the team can do better than you. If someone else can do the job better than you can, then empower them to make it happen. Even if you have the skill, but another person is capable of doing it at least 80 percent as well as you could, delegate it to them.

Third, what brings the greatest reward? In this last section, list the things you do that bring personal satisfaction. Life is too short not to do some things you love. They keep you passionate. And passion provides the fuel to keep you going.

Activity is not necessarily accomplishment. That's the Law of Priorities. Leaders can't afford to let situations or other people decide for them what is most important. You can't just think inside the box. You may need to reinvent the box—or blow it up.

CASE STUDIES

Read these case studies from the Bible and answer the study questions that follow.

1 What Comes First?

Matthew 15:1–20

1 Then some Pharisees and teachers of the law came to Jesus from Jerusalem and asked, 2 "Why do your disciples break the tradition of the elders? They don't wash their hands before they eat!"

3 Jesus replied, "And why do you break the command of God for the sake of your tradition? 4 For God said, 'Honor your father and mother' and 'Anyone who curses their father or mother is to be put to death.' 5 But you say that if anyone declares that what might have been used to help their father or mother is 'devoted to God,' 6 they are not to 'honor their father or mother' with it. Thus you nullify the word of God for the sake of your tradition. 7 You hypocrites! Isaiah was right when he prophesied about you:

8 "'These people honor me with their lips,
    but their hearts are far from me.
9 They worship me in vain;
    their teachings are merely human rules.'"

10 Jesus called the crowd to him and said, "Listen and understand. 11 What goes into someone's mouth does not defile them, but what comes out of their mouth, that is what defiles them."

12 Then the disciples came to him and asked, "Do you know that the Pharisees were offended when they heard this?"

13 He replied, "Every plant that my heavenly Father has not planted will be pulled up by the roots. 14 Leave them; they are blind guides. If the blind lead the blind, both will fall into a pit."

15 Peter said, "Explain the parable to us."

¹⁶ *"Are you still so dull?" Jesus asked them.* ¹⁷ *"Don't you see that whatever enters the mouth goes into the stomach and then out of the body?* ¹⁸ *But the things that come out of a person's mouth come from the heart, and these defile them.* ¹⁹ *For out of the heart come evil thoughts — murder, adultery, sexual immorality, theft, false testimony, slander.* ²⁰ *These are what defile a person; but eating with unwashed hands does not defile them."*

Study Questions

1. What were the priorities of the Pharisees and teachers of the law? Why were those things important to them?

_____

_____

_____

_____

_____

_____

2. What was Jesus' priority?

_____

_____

_____

_____

_____

3. As a leader, what responsibilities did Jesus have to those who did not follow him? How did he handle those? What responsibilities did he have to those who *did* follow him? How did he handle those?

_____

_____

_____

_____

_____

_____

4. What are the implications of Jesus' remark that his followers should leave their blind guides?

---

2 Two Sisters — Two Perspectives

Luke 10:38–42

38 As Jesus and his disciples were on their way, he came to a village where a woman named Martha opened her home to him. 39 She had a sister called Mary, who sat at the Lord's feet listening to what he said. 40 But Martha was distracted by all the preparations that had to be made. She came to him and asked, "Lord, don't you care that my sister has left me to do the work by myself? Tell her to help me!"

41 "Martha, Martha," the Lord answered, "you are worried and upset about many things, 42 but few things are needed — or indeed only one. Mary has chosen what is better, and it will not be taken away from her."

Study Questions

1. Notice that the passage says Martha "was distracted by all the preparations that had to be made." If the things she was doing *had* to be done, then why were her priorities wrong?

---

2. When Martha said to Jesus, "Lord, don't you care that my sister has left me to do the work by myself? Tell her to help me!" what was the root cause of Martha's outburst?

_____

_____

_____

_____

_____

3. Do you believe the differences between Martha and Mary were due to personality, priorities, family history, personal history, or some other reason? Explain your answer.

_____

_____

_____

_____

_____

4. What is your reaction to Jesus' response to Martha? What does it say about his leadership?

_____

_____

_____

_____

_____

③ The Requirement, Return, and Reward of the Twelve

Acts 6:1–7

[1] *In those days when the number of disciples was increasing, the Hellenistic Jews among them complained against the Hebraic Jews because their widows*

were being overlooked in the daily distribution of food. ² So the Twelve gathered all the disciples together and said, "It would not be right for us to neglect the ministry of the word of God in order to wait on tables. ³ Brothers and sisters, choose seven men from among you who are known to be full of the Spirit and wisdom. We will turn this responsibility over to them ⁴ and will give our attention to prayer and the ministry of the word."

⁵ This proposal pleased the whole group. They chose Stephen, a man full of faith and of the Holy Spirit; also Philip, Procorus, Nicanor, Timon, Parmenas, and Nicolas from Antioch, a convert to Judaism. ⁶ They presented these men to the apostles, who prayed and laid their hands on them.

⁷ So the word of God spread. The number of disciples in Jerusalem increased rapidly, and a large number of priests became obedient to the faith.

Study Questions

1. When the Twelve received the complaint, do you think they immediately knew what their response would be? Or do you think they had to discuss their priorities among themselves before they gathered the group together with their direction? Explain your answer.

_____

_____

_____

_____

_____

_____

2. In what other ways could the Twelve have responded? Are any of your alternative solutions better than theirs?

_____

_____

_____

_____

_____

_____

_____

3. What priority-based decisions did the Twelve make in the passage? List as many as you can find.

_____

_____

_____

_____

_____

4. Why do you think the Twelve delegated the selection of the seven to the entire group of the disciples?

_____

_____

_____

_____

_____

_____

LEADERSHIP INSIGHT AND REFLECTION

Based on the reading, what would you say a follower of Christ's priorities should be?

_____

_____

_____

_____

_____

_____

_____

_____

_____

_____

How do those priorities relate to your life and leadership? Are you aligned with them?
Which are you violating?

_____

_____

_____

_____

_____

_____

_____

_____

_____

_____

TAKING ACTION

How is God asking you to change your priorities as his follower? As a leader? List them.

_____

_____

_____

_____

_____

_____

_____

_____

_____

What can you do *today* to align yourself more fully with Christ as a person and as a leader?

_____

_____

_____

_____

_____

_____

_____

GROUP DISCUSSION QUESTIONS

1. What were the Pharisees and teachers of the law trying to do when they confronted Jesus?

2. What was the source of the Pharisees and teachers' priorities? What can you learn from their mistakes?

3. Do you relate more to Martha or Mary? Explain your answer. How has your mindset impacted your leadership?

4. What is the "one thing" Jesus was referring to when talking about Mary? How can you apply this one thing to your leadership?

5. Think about your work as a leader. How much time and effort do you spend in each of these three areas?

   - *Requirement:* What is required of you? These are the things that only you can do.
   - *Return:* What gives you the greatest return? These tasks are the best use of your time.
   - *Reward:* What gives you the greatest reward? These are the tasks you most enjoy.

6. What percentage of your time and effort do you spend on things outside of these three areas?

7. What change do you believe God is asking you to make in your priorities? When will you make the change?

LESSON 18

THE LAW OF SACRIFICE

A Leader Must Give Up to Go Up

DEFINITION OF THE LAW

There is a common misperception that leadership is all about position, perks, and power. Many people today want to climb up the corporate ladder because they believe that freedom, power, and wealth are the prizes waiting at the top. The life of a leader can look glamorous to people on the outside. But the reality is that a leader must give up to go up. In other words, the higher you climb in leadership, the more you should be willing to give up. The heart of good leadership is sacrifice. Here are some truths about sacrifice that every leader should embrace:

There is no success without sacrifice. Every person who has achieved any success in life has made sacrifices to do so. Many invest four or more years and thousands of dollars in a college education to acquire the skills they need for their career. Athletes sacrifice countless hours in the gym and on the practice field preparing to play at a high level. Parents give up much of their free time and resources in order to do a good job raising their children. Life is a series of trades, one thing for another. Nowhere is this more true than in leadership. Effective leaders sacrifice much that is good in order to dedicate themselves to what is best. That's the way the Law of Sacrifice works.

Leaders are often asked to give up more than others. The heart of true leadership is putting your followers ahead of yourself. For that reason, the best leaders give up their rights. As you move up in leadership, your options and rights actually decrease. With each new responsibility you accept, the fewer options you have.

You must keep giving up to stay up. Many people are willing to make sacrifices early in their leadership career. They'll take an undesirable territory to make a name for themselves in the role. They'll move their family to a less desirable city to accept a better position. They'll take a temporary cut in pay for greater opportunities for advancement. The danger is for leaders to ever conclude that they have earned the right to stop sacrificing. In leadership, sacrifice is an ongoing process, not a one-time payment. Today's success is the greatest threat to tomorrow's success. And what gets a team to the top isn't what keeps it there. Leadership success requires continual change, constant improvement, and ongoing sacrifice.

A sacrifice is always made. Anytime you see success, you can be sure someone made sacrifices to make it possible. Whenever you sacrifice, even if you don't witness the success, you can be sure that someone in the future will benefit. The reverse is true. If you have gained any success without your own sacrifice, it's because you're standing on the shoulders of those who sacrificed before you.

The greatest leaders have always been willing to give up to go up, and to keep giving up. They know that success comes from sacrifice. And the value of a leader's sacrifice is that it has the potential to create success for others and even change the world. When leaders give up their rights, the team wins. That's the Law of Sacrifice.

CASE STUDIES

Read these case studies from the Bible and answer the study questions that follow.

❶ Choosing to be Set Apart

Numbers 6:1–21

¹ The LORD said to Moses, ² "Speak to the Israelites and say to them: 'If a man or woman wants to make a special vow, a vow of dedication to the LORD as a Nazirite, ³ they must abstain from wine and other fermented drink and must not drink vinegar made from wine or other fermented drink. They must not drink grape juice or eat grapes or raisins. ⁴ As long as they remain under their Nazirite vow, they must not eat anything that comes from the grapevine, not even the seeds or skins.

⁵ *"'During the entire period of their Nazirite vow, no razor may be used on their head. They must be holy until the period of their dedication to the L*ORD *is over; they must let their hair grow long.*

⁶ *"'Throughout the period of their dedication to the L*ORD*, the Nazirite must not go near a dead body. ⁷ Even if their own father or mother or brother or sister dies, they must not make themselves ceremonially unclean on account of them, because the symbol of their dedication to God is on their head.*
⁸ *Throughout the period of their dedication, they are consecrated to the L*ORD*.*

⁹ *"'If someone dies suddenly in the Nazirite's presence, thus defiling the hair that symbolizes their dedication, they must shave their head on the seventh day—the day of their cleansing. ¹⁰ Then on the eighth day they must bring two doves or two young pigeons to the priest at the entrance to the tent of meeting. ¹¹ The priest is to offer one as a sin offering and the other as a burnt offering to make atonement for the Nazirite because they sinned by being in the presence of the dead body. That same day they are to consecrate their head again. ¹² They must rededicate themselves to the L*ORD *for the same period of dedication and must bring a year-old male lamb as a guilt offering. The previous days do not count, because they became defiled during their period of dedication.*

¹³ *"'Now this is the law of the Nazirite when the period of their dedication is over. They are to be brought to the entrance to the tent of meeting.*
¹⁴ *There they are to present their offerings to the L*ORD*: a year-old male lamb without defect for a burnt offering, a year-old ewe lamb without defect for a sin offering, a ram without defect for a fellowship offering, ¹⁵ together with their grain offerings and drink offerings, and a basket of bread made with the finest flour and without yeast—thick loaves with olive oil mixed in, and thin loaves brushed with olive oil.*

¹⁶ *"'The priest is to present all these before the L*ORD *and make the sin offering and the burnt offering. ¹⁷ He is to present the basket of unleavened bread and is to sacrifice the ram as a fellowship offering to the L*ORD*, together with its grain offering and drink offering.*

18 "'Then at the entrance to the tent of meeting, the Nazirite must shave off the hair that symbolizes their dedication. They are to take the hair and put it in the fire that is under the sacrifice of the fellowship offering.

19 "'After the Nazirite has shaved off the hair that symbolizes their dedication, the priest is to place in their hands a boiled shoulder of the ram, and one thick loaf and one thin loaf from the basket, both made without yeast. 20 The priest shall then wave these before the LORD as a wave offering; they are holy and belong to the priest, together with the breast that was waved and the thigh that was presented. After that, the Nazirite may drink wine.

21 "'This is the law of the Nazirite who vows offerings to the LORD in accordance with their dedication, in addition to whatever else they can afford. They must fulfill the vows they have made, according to the law of the Nazirite.'"

Study Questions

1. Why would anyone desire to take a Nazirite vow?

_____

_____

_____

_____

2. In what ways is a Nazirite vow symbolically similar to the responsibilities of accepting a leadership position?

_____

_____

_____

_____

_____

3. Why do you think a Nazirite who becomes defiled is required to start over again from the beginning? Do you think there is any parallel to this in leadership?

_____

_____

_____

_____

② Paul Declines to Employ His Privileges

1 Corinthians 9:1–23

1 Am I not free? Am I not an apostle? Have I not seen Jesus our Lord? Are you not the result of my work in the Lord? 2 Even though I may not be an apostle to others, surely I am to you! For you are the seal of my apostleship in the Lord.

3 This is my defense to those who sit in judgment on me. 4 Don't we have the right to food and drink? 5 Don't we have the right to take a believing wife along with us, as do the other apostles and the Lord's brothers and Cephas? 6 Or is it only I and Barnabas who lack the right to not work for a living?

7 Who serves as a soldier at his own expense? Who plants a vineyard and does not eat its grapes? Who tends a flock and does not drink the milk? 8 Do I say this merely on human authority? Doesn't the Law say the same thing? 9 For it is written in the Law of Moses: "Do not muzzle an ox while it is treading out the grain." Is it about oxen that God is concerned? 10 Surely he says this for us, doesn't he? Yes, this was written for us, because whoever plows and threshes should be able to do so in the hope of sharing in the harvest. 11 If we have sown spiritual seed among you, is it too much if we reap a material harvest from you? 12 If others have this right of support from you, shouldn't we have it all the more?

But we did not use this right. On the contrary, we put up with anything rather than hinder the gospel of Christ.

13 Don't you know that those who serve in the temple get their food from the temple, and that those who serve at the altar share in what is offered on the altar? 14 In the same way, the Lord has commanded that those who preach the gospel should receive their living from the gospel.

15 But I have not used any of these rights. And I am not writing this in the hope that you will do such things for me, for I would rather die than allow anyone to deprive me of this boast. 16 For when I preach the gospel, I cannot boast, since I am compelled to preach. Woe to me if I do not preach the gospel! 17 If I preach voluntarily, I have a reward; if not voluntarily, I am simply discharging the trust committed to me. 18 What then is my reward? Just this: that in preaching the gospel I may offer it free of charge, and so not make full use of my rights as a preacher of the gospel.

19 Though I am free and belong to no one, I have made myself a slave to everyone, to win as many as possible. 20 To the Jews I became like a Jew, to win the Jews. To those under the law I became like one under the law (though I myself am not under the law), so as to win those under the law. 21 To those not having the law I became like one not having the law (though I am not free from God's law but am under Christ's law), so as to win those not having the law. 22 To the weak I became weak, to win the weak. I have become all things to all people so that by all possible means I might save some. 23 I do all this for the sake of the gospel, that I may share in its blessings.

Study Questions

1. What are all the privileges Paul says he has a right to as an apostle? List them.

   _____

   _____

   _____

   _____

   _____

2. What sacrifices did Paul say he's made? List them.

   _____

   _____

   _____

   _____

   _____

3. Do you think Paul accomplished more by forgoing his privileges, or do you think he would have made a bigger impact if he had used those privileges? Explain your answer.

   _____

   _____

   _____

   _____

   _____

③ Setting the Bar for Leadership

1 Timothy 3:1–10

¹ Here is a trustworthy saying: Whoever aspires to be an overseer desires a noble task. ² Now the overseer is to be above reproach, faithful to his wife, temperate, self-controlled, respectable, hospitable, able to teach, ³ not given to drunkenness, not violent but gentle, not quarrelsome, not a lover of money. ⁴ He must manage his own family well and see that his children obey him, and he must do so in a manner worthy of full respect. ⁵ (If anyone does not know how to manage his own family, how can he take care of God's church?) ⁶ He must not be a recent convert, or he may become conceited and fall under the same judgment as the devil. ⁷ He must also have a good reputation with outsiders, so that he will not fall into disgrace and into the devil's trap.

⁸ In the same way, deacons are to be worthy of respect, sincere, not indulging in much wine, and not pursuing dishonest gain. ⁹ They must keep hold of the deep truths of the faith with a clear conscience. ¹⁰ They must first be tested; and then if there is nothing against them, let them serve as deacons.

Study Questions

1. The term *overseer* is also translated as *elder* or *bishop*. No matter how it is translated, it is a leadership position, and Paul's letter to Timothy makes it clear that the desire to be a leader is a noble aspiration. Why do you think Paul listed criteria for leadership?

   _____
   _____
   _____
   _____

2. Note the criteria Paul listed. What sacrifices do you infer that a leader must make in order to qualify to be an overseer?

   _____
   _____
   _____
   _____

3. Why would conceit be a danger for a recent convert being selected to leadership? Is there any application of this concept in secular leadership for inexperienced people being selected for leadership? Explain.

_____

_____

_____

_____

_____

4. Why does Paul insist on a leader having a good reputation with outsiders? How important is that for secular leadership? Explain.

_____

_____

_____

_____

LEADERSHIP INSIGHT AND REFLECTION

What rights and privileges have you earned or been given to you as a leader?

_____

_____

_____

_____

_____

When and how do you use those rights and privileges?

_____

_____

_____

_____

_____

Are there criteria for effective leadership that you know you are not meeting? If so, what are they? And how are you falling short?

_____

_____

_____

_____

_____

_____

TAKING ACTION

Are there things you should be giving up or forgoing in order to improve as a leader or to better serve your team or organization? What sacrifices should you be making?

_____

_____

_____

_____

_____

_____

Do you find it difficult to make such sacrifices? If so, why? What benefits can you list to help prompt you to make them?

_____

_____

_____

_____

_____

_____

What sacrificial change will you make immediately for the sake of others?

_____

_____

_____

_____

GROUP DISCUSSION QUESTIONS

1. What is your reaction to all the intricacies of the requirements for a Nazirite vow? Can you relate to it at all? Explain.

2. How difficult do you think it was for Paul to set aside his rights and privileges as an apostle as he followed God's calling?

3. Paul's first letter to the Corinthians was prompted primarily by their bad conduct. As a gifted and called leader wanting to address this, how would you have handled it?

4. When you read the criteria for an overseer in Paul's first letter to Timothy, does the bar seem too high, too low, or just right? Explain your answer.

5. Do you tend to place a higher standard for leadership on yourself than others do, or do others place a higher standard on you than you do on yourself? Explain your answer. What are the implications of your answer about you and about your organization?

6. What sacrifice do you feel God is prompting you to make so that you can lead more effectively? Why do you believe you are being asked to make it?

7. What change will you make in response to God? When and how will you make it?

LESSON 19

THE LAW OF TIMING

When to Lead Is as Important as What to Do and Where to Go

DEFINITION OF THE LAW

It's possible for leaders to have a great vision and put off taking action until it's too late to implement it. Or they might know exactly where the team should go next but fail to take them there because they impatiently tried to pull people before they were ready. In both examples, the leaders had great vision but horrible timing. Timing often makes the difference between success and failure in an endeavor. Often, it truly is everything. When to lead is as important as what to do and where to go. That's the Law of Timing. Here's how it plays out in leadership: Every time a leader makes a move, there are really only four outcomes:

The wrong action at the wrong time leads to disaster. Bad ideas plus bad timing equal bad results. This is pretty obvious, but it should never be ignored. An effective leader is sure of both the what and the when. Only then does he take action. When disaster strikes, the team suffers. And so does your leadership.

The right action at the wrong time results in resistance. No matter how convinced you are of the perfection of your plans, if you try to introduce or implement them before your people are ready, you will encounter pushback. And the harder you try to forge ahead, the more resistance you will face. Leadership often requires a lot of patience. Just because you can see the vision clearly doesn't mean your team is ready to embrace it. Wait and act at the right time.

The wrong action at the right time is a mistake. Some people who are naturally entrepreneurial have a strong sense of timing. They intuitively know when it's time to make a move, and they are eager to take action. They're usually right; there's an opportunity to be seized. But if they haven't yet clarified the vision, they can be so eager to jump in that they make the wrong move. Don't move just for the sake of movement. Wait until you know what to do before you try to do it.

The right action at the right time produces success. Everything just works. The team achieves goals, reaps rewards, and gains momentum. Sometimes, when the right leader takes the right action at the right time, a pivotal moment occurs, and it transforms everything. When you are confident in your vision and sure of the timing, that's when to go for it.

Reading a situation and knowing what to do or where to go are not enough to make you succeed in leadership. If you want your organization, department, or team to move forward, you must pay attention to timing. Only the right action *at the right time* will bring success. Anything else exacts some kind of price. No leader can escape the Law of Timing.

CASE STUDIES

Read these case studies from the Bible and answer the study questions that follow.

① Saul's Bad Decision

1 Samuel 10:1, 5–8

¹ Then Samuel took a flask of olive oil and poured it on Saul's head and kissed him, saying, "Has not the LORD anointed you ruler over his inheritance?...

⁵ "You will go to Gibeah of God, where there is a Philistine outpost. As you approach the town, you will meet a procession of prophets coming down from the high place with lyres, timbrels, pipes and harps being played before them, and they will be prophesying. ⁶ The Spirit of the Lord will come powerfully upon you, and you will prophesy with them; and you will be changed into a different person. ⁷ Once these signs are fulfilled, do whatever your hand finds to do, for God is with you.

⁸ "Go down ahead of me to Gilgal. I will surely come down to you to sacrifice burnt offerings and fellowship offerings, but you must wait seven days until I come to you and tell you what you are to do."

1 Samuel 13:5–14

⁵ The Philistines assembled to fight Israel, with three thousand chariots, six thousand charioteers, and soldiers as numerous as the sand on the seashore. They went up and camped at Mikmash, east of Beth Aven.
⁶ When the Israelites saw that their situation was critical and that their army was hard pressed, they hid in caves and thickets, among the rocks, and in pits and cisterns. ⁷ Some Hebrews even crossed the Jordan to the land of Gad and Gilead.

Saul remained at Gilgal, and all the troops with him were quaking with fear. ⁸ He waited seven days, the time set by Samuel; but Samuel did not come to Gilgal, and Saul's men began to scatter. ⁹ So he said, "Bring me the burnt offering and the fellowship offerings." And Saul offered up the burnt offering. ¹⁰ Just as he finished making the offering, Samuel arrived, and Saul went out to greet him.

¹¹ "What have you done?" asked Samuel.

Saul replied, "When I saw that the men were scattering, and that you did not come at the set time, and that the Philistines were assembling at Mikmash, ¹² I thought, 'Now the Philistines will come down against me at Gilgal, and I have not sought the Lord's favor.' So I felt compelled to offer the burnt offering."

¹³ "You have done a foolish thing," Samuel said. "You have not kept the command the Lord your God gave you; if you had, he would have established your kingdom over Israel for all time. ¹⁴ But now your kingdom will not endure; the Lord has sought out a man after his own heart and appointed him ruler of his people, because you have not kept the Lord's command."

Study Questions

1. What motivated Saul to offer the burnt offerings himself?

   _____

   _____

   _____

   _____

   _____

2. Most people admire proactive leaders who make things happen. Why were Saul's actions wrong?

   _____

   _____

   _____

   _____

   _____

3. What was the cost of Saul's violation of the Law of Timing?

   _____

   _____

   _____

   _____

   _____

❷ An Entire Nation's Fate Rests on Her Timing

Esther 3:13–14

[13] *Dispatches were sent by couriers to all the king's provinces with the order to destroy, kill and annihilate all the Jews—young and old, women and children—on a single day, the thirteenth day of the twelfth month, the month of Adar, and to plunder their goods.* [14] *A copy of the text of the edict was to be issued as law in every province and made known to the people of every nationality so they would be ready for that day.*

Esther 4:1–16

1 When Mordecai learned of all that had been done, he tore his clothes, put on sackcloth and ashes, and went out into the city, wailing loudly and bitterly. 2 But he went only as far as the king's gate, because no one clothed in sackcloth was allowed to enter it. 3 In every province to which the edict and order of the king came, there was great mourning among the Jews, with fasting, weeping and wailing. Many lay in sackcloth and ashes.

4 When Esther's eunuchs and female attendants came and told her about Mordecai, she was in great distress. She sent clothes for him to put on instead of his sackcloth, but he would not accept them. 5 Then Esther summoned Hathak, one of the king's eunuchs assigned to attend her, and ordered him to find out what was troubling Mordecai and why.

6 So Hathak went out to Mordecai in the open square of the city in front of the king's gate. 7 Mordecai told him everything that had happened to him, including the exact amount of money Haman had promised to pay into the royal treasury for the destruction of the Jews. 8 He also gave him a copy of the text of the edict for their annihilation, which had been published in Susa, to show to Esther and explain it to her, and he told him to instruct her to go into the king's presence to beg for mercy and plead with him for her people.

9 Hathak went back and reported to Esther what Mordecai had said. 10 Then she instructed him to say to Mordecai, 11 "All the king's officials and the people of the royal provinces know that for any man or woman who approaches the king in the inner court without being summoned the king has but one law: that they be put to death unless the king extends the gold scepter to them and spares their lives. But thirty days have passed since I was called to go to the king."

12 When Esther's words were reported to Mordecai, 13 he sent back this answer: "Do not think that because you are in the king's house you alone of all the Jews will escape. 14 For if you remain silent at this time, relief and deliverance for the Jews will arise from another place, but you and your father's family will perish. And who knows but that you have come to your royal position for such a time as this?"

15 Then Esther sent this reply to Mordecai: 16 "Go, gather together all the Jews who are in Susa, and fast for me. Do not eat or drink for three days, night or day. I and my attendants will fast as you do. When this is done, I will go to the king, even though it is against the law. And if I perish, I perish."

Study Questions

1. What role does courage play when it comes to timing in leadership?

_____

_____

_____

_____

2. Does it take more courage to wait or to take action? Explain your answer.

_____

_____

_____

_____

3. Much of the timing in Esther's situation was out of her control. What things within her control did she do to try to make her timing advantageous?

_____

_____

_____

_____

③ Jesus Waited for the Right Time

John 7:1–15

¹ After this, Jesus went around in Galilee. He did not want to go about in Judea because the Jewish leaders there were looking for a way to kill him. ² But when the Jewish Festival of Tabernacles was near, ³ Jesus' brothers said to him, "Leave Galilee and go to Judea, so that your disciples there may see the works you do. ⁴ No one who wants to become a public figure acts in secret. Since you are doing these things, show yourself to the world." ⁵ For even his own brothers did not believe in him.

⁶ Therefore Jesus told them, "My time is not yet here; for you any time will do. ⁷ The world cannot hate you, but it hates me because I testify that its works are evil. ⁸ You go to the festival. I am not going up to this festival, because my time has not yet fully come." ⁹ After he had said this, he stayed in Galilee.

¹⁰ However, after his brothers had left for the festival, he went also, not publicly, but in secret.

¹¹ Now at the festival the Jewish leaders were watching for Jesus and asking, "Where is he?"

¹² Among the crowds there was widespread whispering about him. Some said, "He is a good man."

Others replied, "No, he deceives the people." ¹³ But no one would say anything publicly about him for fear of the leaders.

¹⁴ Not until halfway through the festival did Jesus go up to the temple courts and begin to teach. ¹⁵ The Jews there were amazed and asked, "How did this man get such learning without having been taught?"

Study Questions

1. Why did Jesus' brothers try to push him into going to Jerusalem for the Festival of Tabernacles? What was their motivation? What was Jesus' motivation?

   _____

   _____

   _____

   _____

2. What do you think Jesus meant when he said it was not yet fully his time? Explain.

   _____

   _____

   _____

   _____

3. Why do you believe Jesus waited, and then went to Jerusalem anyway not long afterward? What difference did that timing make? Was he trying to connect with some people and avoid others?

_____

_____

_____

_____

_____

_____

4. Jesus waited until halfway through the festival to begin teaching. What impact did that timing have?

_____

_____

_____

_____

_____

LEADERSHIP INSIGHT AND REFLECTION

What criteria did each of the leaders use to determine timing in the passages you read? Which criteria were good, and which were not? Why?

_____

_____

_____

_____

_____

_____

_____

_____

_____

_____

How do you judge the timing of your actions as a leader? What criteria do you use to decide when to act and when to wait? List as many criteria as you can here:

_____

_____

_____

_____

_____

_____

_____

Go back over the list you made in response to the last question. On a scale from 1 (ineffective) to 10 (highly effective), rate each. What do the low-scoring criteria have in common? What do the high-scoring criteria have in common?

_____

_____

_____

_____

_____

_____

TAKING ACTION

Based on your analysis of your criteria for timing, what do you need to change to become better at practicing the Law of Timing? What will you do and when will you do it?

_____

_____

_____

_____

_____

_____

_____

GROUP DISCUSSION QUESTIONS

1. Why do you believe Samuel was so specific about what Saul was to do? And why was he so harsh in his response?

2. What do you think would have happened if Saul had continued to wait as he was instructed and let Samuel make the sacrifices? How might that have changed the rest of Israel's history?

3. Jesus told his brothers that any timing would do for them. What did he mean by that?

4. In what ways did emotions impact the leaders' judgment of timing in the three passages? Did emotions help leaders to make good timing choices or poor ones?

5. As a leader, what criteria do you think are important for judging what to do and when to do it?

6. What changes in your leadership do you believe God is asking you to make so that you can become better at the Law of Timing?

7. How difficult will those changes be for you to make? How will you go about initiating them?

THE LAW OF EXPLOSIVE GROWTH

To Add Growth, Lead Followers— To Multiply, Lead Leaders

DEFINITION OF THE LAW

Most leaders are impatient. They want to see the vision fulfilled. They delight in progress. Good leaders quickly assess where an organization is, project where it needs to go, and have strong ideas about how to get it there. The problem is that most of the time the people and the organization lag behind the leader. For that reason, leaders always feel a tension between where they and their people *are* and where they *ought to be*.

How do you relieve that tension between where the organization is and where you want it to be? The answer can be found in the Law of Explosive Growth: (1) If you develop yourself, you can experience personal success; (2) If you develop a team, your organization can experience growth; and (3) If you develop leaders, your organization can achieve explosive growth.

Leaders who attract followers but never develop leaders get tired. Why? Because they themselves must deal with every person under their authority. Being able to impact only the people you can touch personally is very limiting. Leaders who attract followers grow their organization only one person at a time. When you attract one follower, you impact one person. And you receive the value and power of one person. However, leaders who develop leaders multiply their organization's growth, because for every leader they develop, they also receive the value of all of that leader's followers. And the better the leaders they develop, the greater the quality and quantity of followers and the greater the reach.

Becoming a leader who develops leaders requires an entirely different focus and attitude from simply attracting and leading followers. To multiply your impact through leadership development, here are two ways to change your focus:

Develop those with the most potential. Ironically, these top performers are often the ones who demand the least amount of your time and attention. But you need to intentionally pursue your team members with the greatest leadership potential—and give the majority of your time and attention to them. If you develop the best, the best will help with the rest.

Develop people's strengths. When you're trying to help someone grow, it's tempting to devote the most effort to shoring up their weaknesses. After all, weaknesses are usually much more noticeable and problematic than strengths. And certain weaknesses—like those of character—must be addressed. But the most strategic way to develop leaders is to equip them to grow the most in their areas of strength. The result is much more improvement and impact.

Leadership development compounds. The more you invest in potential leaders and the longer you do it, the greater the growth and the higher the return. Developing leaders creates an incredible multiplication effect in an organization that can be achieved in no other way—not by increasing resources, reducing costs, increasing profit margins, improving systems, implementing quality procedures, or doing anything else. That's the incredible power of the Law of Explosive Growth.

CASE STUDIES

Read these case studies from the Bible and answer the study questions that follow.

Leading an Army of Craftsmen

Exodus 35:30–35

30 Then Moses said to the Israelites, "See, the LORD has chosen Bezalel son of Uri, the son of Hur, of the tribe of Judah, 31 and he has filled him with the

Spirit of God, with wisdom, with understanding, with knowledge and with all kinds of skills— *32 to make artistic designs for work in gold, silver and bronze, 33 to cut and set stones, to work in wood and to engage in all kinds of artistic crafts. 34 And he has given both him and Oholiab son of Ahisamak, of the tribe of Dan, the ability to teach others. 35 He has filled them with skill to do all kinds of work as engravers, designers, embroiderers in blue, purple and scarlet yarn and fine linen, and weavers—all of them skilled workers and designers.*

Exodus 36:1–3

1 "So Bezalel, Oholiab and every skilled person to whom the LORD has given skill and ability to know how to carry out all the work of constructing the sanctuary are to do the work just as the LORD has commanded."

2 Then Moses summoned Bezalel and Oholiab and every skilled person to whom the LORD had given ability and who was willing to come and do the work. 3 They received from Moses all the offerings the Israelites had brought to carry out the work of constructing the sanctuary.

Exodus 39:32–43

32 So all the work on the tabernacle, the tent of meeting, was completed. The Israelites did everything just as the LORD commanded Moses. 33 Then they brought the tabernacle to Moses: the tent and all its furnishings, its clasps, frames, crossbars, posts and bases; 34 the covering of ram skins dyed red and the covering of another durable leather and the shielding curtain; 35 the ark of the covenant law with its poles and the atonement cover; 36 the table with all its articles and the bread of the Presence; 37 the pure gold lampstand with its row of lamps and all its accessories, and the olive oil for the light; 38 the gold altar, the anointing oil, the fragrant incense, and the curtain for the entrance to the tent; 39 the bronze altar with its bronze grating, its poles and all its utensils; the basin with its stand; 40 the curtains of the courtyard with its posts and bases, and the curtain for the entrance to the courtyard; the ropes and tent pegs for the courtyard; all the furnishings for the tabernacle, the tent of meeting; 41 and the woven garments worn for ministering in the sanctuary, both the sacred garments for Aaron the priest and the garments for his sons when serving as priests.

⁴² The Israelites had done all the work just as the Lᴏʀᴅ had commanded Moses. ⁴³ Moses inspected the work and saw that they had done it just as the Lᴏʀᴅ had commanded. So Moses blessed them.

Study Questions

1. God gave Moses specific instructions about the construction of the tabernacle and all of the objects related to it, including the ark of the covenant. How much trust did it require for him to delegate the construction of all those objects to Bezalel and Oholiab?

   _____

   _____

   _____

   _____

2. Having read the list of items created and that Moses summoned every skilled person to whom the Lord had given ability and who was willing to come and do the work, how many people would you guess worked on this project? How would you speculate Bezalel and Oholiab handled the leadership of all those craftsmen?

   _____

   _____

   _____

   _____

   _____

3. How do you think things would have turned out if Moses had attempted to direct the craftsmen himself instead of enlisting the leadership of Bezalel and Oholiab?

   _____

   _____

   _____

② Leaders in Training

Luke 10:1–12, 16–21

¹ *After this the Lord appointed seventy-two others and sent them two by two ahead of him to every town and place where he was about to go.* ² *He told them, "The harvest is plentiful, but the workers are few. Ask the Lord of the harvest, therefore, to send out workers into his harvest field.* ³ *Go! I am sending you out like lambs among wolves.* ⁴ *Do not take a purse or bag or sandals; and do not greet anyone on the road.*

⁵ *"When you enter a house, first say, 'Peace to this house.'* ⁶ *If someone who promotes peace is there, your peace will rest on them; if not, it will return to you.* ⁷ *Stay there, eating and drinking whatever they give you, for the worker deserves his wages. Do not move around from house to house.*

⁸ *"When you enter a town and are welcomed, eat what is offered to you.* ⁹ *Heal the sick who are there and tell them, 'The kingdom of God has come near to you.'* ¹⁰ *But when you enter a town and are not welcomed, go into its streets and say,* ¹¹ *'Even the dust of your town we wipe from our feet as a warning to you. Yet be sure of this: The kingdom of God has come near.'* ¹² *I tell you, it will be more bearable on that day for Sodom than for that town. . . .*

¹⁶ *"Whoever listens to you listens to me; whoever rejects you rejects me; but whoever rejects me rejects him who sent me."*

¹⁷ *The seventy-two returned with joy and said, "Lord, even the demons submit to us in your name."*

¹⁸ *He replied, "I saw Satan fall like lightning from heaven.* ¹⁹ *I have given you authority to trample on snakes and scorpions and to overcome all the power of the enemy; nothing will harm you.* ²⁰ *However, do not rejoice that the spirits submit to you, but rejoice that your names are written in heaven."*

²¹ *At that time Jesus, full of joy through the Holy Spirit, said, "I praise you, Father, Lord of heaven and earth, because you have hidden these things from the wise and learned, and revealed them to little children. Yes, Father, for this is what you were pleased to do.*

Study Questions

1. The first time Jesus sent people out to preach and heal the sick, he chose the twelve apostles (Luke 9). This passage doesn't explain how Jesus selected the seventy-two leaders. What criteria would you speculate Jesus used?

_____

_____

_____

_____

_____

2. Why did Jesus give the seventy-two leaders such detailed instructions?

_____

_____

_____

_____

_____

3. When the seventy-two returned to Jesus, where was their focus? Why do you think Jesus responded to them the way he did?

_____

_____

_____

_____

_____

4. Jesus also revealed that he was giving these leaders additional authority and power—to overcome all the power of the enemy. Why did Jesus tell them this?

_____

_____

_____

_____

_____

③ Paul's Strategy for Growth

Acts 14:20–23

20 The next day he [Paul] and Barnabas left for Derbe.
21 They preached the gospel in that city and won a large number of disciples. Then they returned to Lystra, Iconium and Antioch,
22 strengthening the disciples and encouraging them to remain true to the faith. "We must go through many hardships to enter the kingdom of God," they said. 23 Paul and Barnabas appointed elders for them in each church and, with prayer and fasting, committed them to the Lord, in whom they had put their trust.

2 Timothy 2:1–2

1 You then, my son, be strong in the grace that is in Christ Jesus. 2 And the things you have heard me say in the presence of many witnesses entrust to reliable people who will also be qualified to teach others.

Titus 1:1–5

1 Paul, a servant of God and an apostle of Jesus Christ to further the faith of God's elect and their knowledge of the truth that leads to godliness—
2 in the hope of eternal life, which God, who does not lie, promised before the beginning of time, 3 and which now at his appointed season he has brought to light through the preaching entrusted to me by the command of God our Savior,
4 To Titus, my true son in our common faith:
Grace and peace from God the Father and Christ Jesus our Savior.
5 The reason I left you in Crete was that you might put in order what was left unfinished and appoint elders in every town, as I directed you.

Study Questions

1. Why did Paul and Barnabas appoint elders in every church in Derbe?

   _____

   _____

   _____

   _____

   _____

   _____

2. What do you learn about Paul from his greeting to Titus? Why does he include his credentials?

   _____

   _____

   _____

   _____

   _____

   _____

3. What are the leadership implications of Paul's comment that he left Titus in Crete to appoint elders in every town? What does that imply about Titus' leadership? What does it say about Paul's confidence in him?

   _____

   _____

   _____

   _____

   _____

4. What do the instructions to Timothy reveal about Paul's strategy for developing leaders?

   _____

   _____

   _____

   _____

   _____

LEADERSHIP INSIGHT AND REFLECTION

What do Moses, Jesus, and Paul have in common in these passages as they practiced the Law of Explosive Growth?

_____

_____

_____

_____

_____

_____

How did their leadership practices expand and multiply their impact?

_____

_____

_____

_____

_____

TAKING ACTION

Based on your observations of these three leaders, where do you most need to grow as a leader to effectively practice the Law of Explosive Growth? What most often holds you back from leading leaders? How much can you change to improve? What specific steps can you take immediately?

_____

_____

_____

_____

_____

_____

_____

GROUP DISCUSSION QUESTIONS

1. Knowing how specific God's instructions were and how important the tabernacle would be, how would you have responded to being given the responsibility for creating it and all of the associated objects?

2. What insights did you gain about Jesus and his way of leading leaders from the instructions he gave the seventy-two and his debriefing conversation after they returned?

3. What were the two qualities Paul told Timothy his leaders must have? Why were each of those qualities important?

4. As Moses selected Bezalel and Oholiab, they had one big specific task to accomplish. The leaders chosen by Jesus and Paul had a long-term mission to accomplish. How did the selection of leaders differ?

5. What leadership development practices can you adopt from the examples of Moses, Jesus, and Paul?

6. What was your greatest takeaway from this lesson?

7. How do you believe God is asking you to change? When and how will you do it?

THE LAW OF LEGACY

A Leader's Lasting Value Is Measured by Succession

DEFINITION OF THE LAW

What do you want people to say at your funeral? That may seem like an odd question. But if you want your leadership to really have meaning, you need to think about what will be said at your eulogy or written on your tombstone—in other words, your "life sentence." Figuring this out not only sets the direction for your life, but it also determines the legacy you will leave. All the success you've achieved up until today doesn't count for much if you leave nothing behind. A leader's lasting value is measured by succession. That's the Law of Legacy.

Every person leaves some kind of legacy. For some it's positive. For others it's negative. But we have a choice regarding the legacy we will leave, and we must work and be intentional to make it happen. Here's how:

Declare it. Most people simply accept their lives—they don't lead them. They let themselves be swept along by the current, but they never check to make sure they're in the correct channel. By investing some thought into the impact you want to leave after you're gone, you'll point yourself in the best direction and improve your chance of making it a reality.

Live it out. For your legacy to actually happen in the future, it needs to begin right now, with you. You have to live it out through your own leadership. Wisdom comes from experience. You can't pass on knowledge and experience that you don't have. You must create now what you want others to sustain.

Prepare your successor. Effective leaders work to develop other leaders. The only time you have to do that is now. Invest as much time as possible in equipping the person who will succeed you. The more they learn from you personally, the more likely they are to maintain your legacy once they take the leadership role.

Don't forget to pass the baton. The most important part of a relay race is the exchange. That's where the runners must pass the baton to their teammates. You can have the fastest runners in the world—each one a record setter—but if they blow the exchange, they lose the race. The same is true when it comes to the Law of Legacy. No matter how well you lead or how good your successor is, if you don't correctly pass the baton, you will not leave the legacy you desire. Whether you pass it before the other person is ready, or hold onto it for too long, a bad exchange can weaken or even irrevocably damage your legacy.

Just about anybody can make an organization look good for a moment—by launching a flashy new program or product, drawing crowds to a big event, or slashing the budget to boost the bottom line. But when all is said and done, your ability as a leader will not be judged by what you achieved personally. Leaders are always judged by how well the people they invest in carry on after they are gone. A leader's lasting value is measured by succession.

CASE STUDIES

Read these case studies from the Bible and answer the study questions that follow.

① David Establishes Solomon as His Successor

1 Kings 1:24–48

24 Nathan said, "Have you, my lord the king, declared that Adonijah shall be king after you, and that he will sit on your throne? 25 Today he has gone down and sacrificed great numbers of cattle, fattened calves, and sheep. He has invited all the king's sons, the commanders of the army and Abiathar the priest. Right now they are eating and drinking with him and saying, 'Long live King Adonijah!' 26 But me your servant, and Zadok the priest, and Benaiah son of Jehoiada, and your servant Solomon he did not invite. 27 Is this something my lord the king has done without letting his servants know who should sit on the throne of my lord the king after him?"

28 Then King David said, "Call in Bathsheba." So she came into the king's presence and stood before him.

29 The king then took an oath: "As surely as the LORD lives, who has delivered me out of every trouble, 30 I will surely carry out this very day what I swore to you by the LORD, the God of Israel: Solomon your son shall be king after me, and he will sit on my throne in my place."

31 Then Bathsheba bowed down with her face to the ground, prostrating herself before the king, and said, "May my lord King David live forever!"

32 King David said, "Call in Zadok the priest, Nathan the prophet and Benaiah son of Jehoiada." When they came before the king, 33 he said to them: "Take your lord's servants with you and have Solomon my son mount my own mule and take him down to Gihon. 34 There have Zadok the priest and Nathan the prophet anoint him king over Israel. Blow the trumpet and shout, 'Long live King Solomon!' 35 Then you are to go up with him, and he is to come and sit on my throne and reign in my place. I have appointed him ruler over Israel and Judah."

36 Benaiah son of Jehoiada answered the king, "Amen! May the LORD, the God of my lord the king, so declare it. 37 As the LORD was with my lord the king, so may he be with Solomon to make his throne even greater than the throne of my lord King David!"

38 So Zadok the priest, Nathan the prophet, Benaiah son of Jehoiada, the Kerethites and the Pelethites went down and had Solomon mount King David's mule, and they escorted him to Gihon. 39 Zadok the priest took the horn of oil from the sacred tent and anointed Solomon. Then they sounded the trumpet and all the people shouted, "Long live King Solomon!" 40 And all the people went up after him, playing pipes and rejoicing greatly, so that the ground shook with the sound.

41 Adonijah and all the guests who were with him heard it as they were finishing their feast. On hearing the sound of the trumpet, Joab asked, "What's the meaning of all the noise in the city?"

42 Even as he was speaking, Jonathan son of Abiathar the priest arrived. Adonijah said, "Come in. A worthy man like you must be bringing good news."

43 "Not at all!" Jonathan answered. "Our lord King David has made Solomon king. 44 The king has sent with him Zadok the priest, Nathan the prophet, Benaiah son of Jehoiada, the Kerethites and the Pelethites, and they have put him on the king's mule, 45 and Zadok the priest and Nathan the prophet have anointed him king at Gihon. From there they have gone up cheering, and the city resounds with it. That's the noise you hear. 46 Moreover, Solomon has taken his seat on the royal throne. 47 Also, the royal officials have come to congratulate our lord King David, saying, 'May your God make Solomon's name more famous than yours and his throne greater than yours!' And the king bowed in worship on his bed 48 and said, 'Praise be to the LORD, the God of Israel, who has allowed my eyes to see a successor on my throne today.'"

1 Kings 2:1–4

1 When the time drew near for David to die, he gave a charge to Solomon his son.

2 "I am about to go the way of all the earth," he said. "So be strong, act like a man, 3 and observe what the LORD your God requires: Walk in obedience to him, and keep his decrees and commands, his laws and regulations, as written in the Law of Moses. Do this so that you may prosper in all you do and wherever you go 4 and that the LORD may keep his promise to me: 'If your descendants watch how they live, and if they walk faithfully before me with all their heart and soul, you will never fail to have a successor on the throne of Israel.'

Study Questions

1. Does David bear any responsibility for Adonijah's attempt to ascend the throne on his own initiative? Explain.

   _____

   _____

   _____

   _____

   _____

2. The passage goes on to say after Solomon was put on the throne, Adonijah pleaded with Solomon for mercy, and when it was granted, Adonijah bowed to Solomon (see 1 Kings 1:50–53). Why did David's strategy work?

_____

_____

_____

_____

3. As David approached death and gave Solomon advice, what was he attempting to do?

_____

_____

_____

_____

② Elijah Chooses Elisha

1 Kings 19:19–21

¹⁹ So Elijah went from there and found Elisha son of Shaphat. He was plowing with twelve yoke of oxen, and he himself was driving the twelfth pair. Elijah went up to him and threw his cloak around him. ²⁰ Elisha then left his oxen and ran after Elijah. "Let me kiss my father and mother goodbye," he said, "and then I will come with you."

"Go back," Elijah replied. "What have I done to you?"

²¹ So Elisha left him and went back. He took his yoke of oxen and slaughtered them. He burned the plowing equipment to cook the meat and gave it to the people, and they ate. Then he set out to follow Elijah and became his servant.

2 Kings 2:8–15

⁸ Elijah took his cloak, rolled it up and struck the water with it. The water divided to the right and to the left, and the two of them crossed over on dry ground.

⁹ When they had crossed, Elijah said to Elisha, "Tell me, what can I do for you before I am taken from you?"

"Let me inherit a double portion of your spirit," Elisha replied.

¹⁰ "You have asked a difficult thing," Elijah said, "yet if you see me when I am taken from you, it will be yours—otherwise, it will not."

¹¹ As they were walking along and talking together, suddenly a chariot of fire and horses of fire appeared and separated the two of them, and Elijah went up to heaven in a whirlwind. ¹² Elisha saw this and cried out, "My father! My father! The chariots and horsemen of Israel!" And Elisha saw him no more. Then he took hold of his garment and tore it in two.

¹³ Elisha then picked up Elijah's cloak that had fallen from him and went back and stood on the bank of the Jordan. ¹⁴ He took the cloak that had fallen from Elijah and struck the water with it. "Where now is the Lᴏʀᴅ, the God of Elijah?" he asked. When he struck the water, it divided to the right and to the left, and he crossed over.

¹⁵ The company of the prophets from Jericho, who were watching, said, "The spirit of Elijah is resting on Elisha." And they went to meet him and bowed to the ground before him.

Study Questions

1. The symbolism of Elijah placing his cloak on Elisha was that he was being chosen as his successor. What was Elisha's response to this?

   _____

   _____

   _____

   _____

2. The passage simply says that Elisha followed Elijah and became his servant. What does this imply about the process a successor may have to go through before taking the place of his leader?

   _____

   _____

   _____

   _____

3. Why do you believe Elijah told Elisha he had to remain and see him when he was taken in order to receive a double portion of his spirit?

_____

_____

_____

_____

_____

4. What do Elisha's actions with Elijah's cloak symbolize?

_____

_____

_____

_____

③ Jesus' Plan of Succession

Luke 6:12–16

¹² One of those days Jesus went out to a mountainside to pray, and spent the night praying to God. ¹³ When morning came, he called his disciples to him and chose twelve of them, whom he also designated apostles: ¹⁴ Simon (whom he named Peter), his brother Andrew, James, John, Philip, Bartholomew, ¹⁵ Matthew, Thomas, James son of Alphaeus, Simon who was called the Zealot, ¹⁶ Judas son of James, and Judas Iscariot, who became a traitor.

Matthew 28:16–20

¹⁶ Then the eleven disciples went to Galilee, to the mountain where Jesus had told them to go. ¹⁷ When they saw him, they worshiped him; but some doubted. ¹⁸ Then Jesus came to them and said, "All authority in heaven and on earth has been given to me. ¹⁹ Therefore go and make disciples of all nations, baptizing them in the name of the Father and of the Son and of the Holy Spirit, ²⁰ and teaching them to obey everything I have commanded you. And surely I am with you always, to the very end of the age."

Study Questions

1. Why do you think Jesus chose twelve people to be apostles? And why did he choose the people he did?

   _____

   _____

   _____

   _____

2. What are the implications of Jesus' statement that all authority in heaven and on earth has been given to him?

   _____

   _____

   _____

   _____

3. What are the importance of the people Jesus chose, the mission he gave them, and the authority he has? Rank them.

   _____

   _____

   _____

   _____

LEADERSHIP INSIGHT AND REFLECTION

Based on where you are in your career or stage of life, do you find it easy or difficult to think about selecting and developing a successor? Explain.

_____

_____

_____

_____

_____

Based on the three passages you read, what stage of the process are you in related to the Law of Legacy?

- Developing your own skills and credibility as a leader
- Attracting and influencing leaders
- Selecting a successor
- Developing and grooming a successor
- Empowering and releasing a successor

What are the challenges of your current stage of the process?

_____
_____
_____
_____

What challenges or obstacles do you anticipate needing to overcome to enter the next stage?

_____
_____
_____
_____

TAKING ACTION

Decide where you need to place your focus—on completing the current stage in the succession process or working toward entering the next one. Then write a plan for completing it.

_____
_____
_____
_____
_____
_____

When will you do it?   Date: _____
What is your target date to complete it?   Date: _____

GROUP DISCUSSION QUESTIONS

1. It appears that David had previously promised to make Solomon his successor, yet Bathsheba's son had not yet been established. What might have been some of the reasons?

2. David's actions related to succession were precipitated by a crisis. How common is that in organizations? How does it usually turn out?

3. How would you have felt being selected as a successor, as Elisha was, and having to wait years to take your place as a leader? What would you have focused on as you were waiting?

4. Even though Elijah selected Elisha, he said his protégé's request for a double portion of his spirit was a difficult thing to grant. Why do you believe he said that? What do you think of Elisha's response?

5. Jesus' command to his followers has been called the Great Commission, and it is still guiding his followers nearly two thousand years later. What has made it so powerful?

6. Where are you in the succession process?

   - Developing your own skills and credibility as a leader
   - Attracting and influencing leaders
   - Selecting a successor
   - Developing and grooming a successor
   - Empowering and releasing a successor

7. Describe what you must do to complete your current stage and prepare for the next.

8. Do you think completing the stages of succession is a one-time process or something to be repeated throughout a leader's lifetime? Explain your answer.

Final Group Discussion Questions

I recommend that you meet together with your group one additional time after you finish the lesson on The Law of Legacy. Before the meeting, ask everyone to take some time to reflect on the entire leadership development process they've gone through. Then when you meet, answer the following questions.

1. How would you describe your leadership journey since you started this process?

2. Have you taken on a greater leadership role or been more proactive as a leader since studying the 21 laws in Scripture? If so, how? If not, why not?

3. Which law did you find that you instinctively practice well? Explain.

4. Which of the laws did you find the most challenging to you personally as a leader? Explain.

5. What big-picture changes have you seen in your leadership philosophy or your approach to leading others?

6. Are others responding to you differently as a leader than in the past? If so, how?

7. What is your single greatest takeaway from this learning process?

8. What did you learn from others in the group?

9. Where do you most want to grow next in your leadership?

ABOUT THE AUTHOR

John C. Maxwell is a #1 *New York Times* bestselling author, coach, and speaker who has sold more than thirty million books in fifty languages. He has been identified as the #1 leader in business by the American Management Association and the most influential leadership expert in the world by *Business Insider* and *Inc.* magazines. He is the founder of the John Maxwell Company, the John Maxwell Team, EQUIP, and the John Maxwell Leadership Foundation, organizations that have trained millions of leaders from every country of the world. The recipient of the Mother Teresa Prize for Global Peace and Leadership from the Luminary Leadership Network, Dr. Maxwell speaks each year to Fortune 500 companies, presidents of nations, and many of the world's top business leaders. He can be followed at Twitter.com/JohnCMaxwell. For more information about him, visit JohnMaxwell.com.

Your Free Daily Video Coaching with John!

MINUTE WITH MAXWELL

John Maxwell's leadership principles are as timeless as they are true. Let John support your success by equipping you with leadership teachings to apply to your life daily.

Sign up to learn and grow everyday...

- **Enjoy wisdom & wit** from world renown leadership expert, John Maxwell.

- The most **powerful video minute** of coaching on the planet.

- **Benefit** from John's 40+ years as one of the world's top communicators **FOR FREE!**

- As a **BONUS,** send John your word, and he will teach on it during one of his videos.

> "I love each word.
>
> **My kids and I listen as we walk to school each morning and then we talk about what we learned. It's a great way for us to set our intention for the day!"**
>
> —Denise Russo, USA

Sign up for your Minute with Maxwell today at
www.JohnMaxwellTeam.com/MWM-DLWY

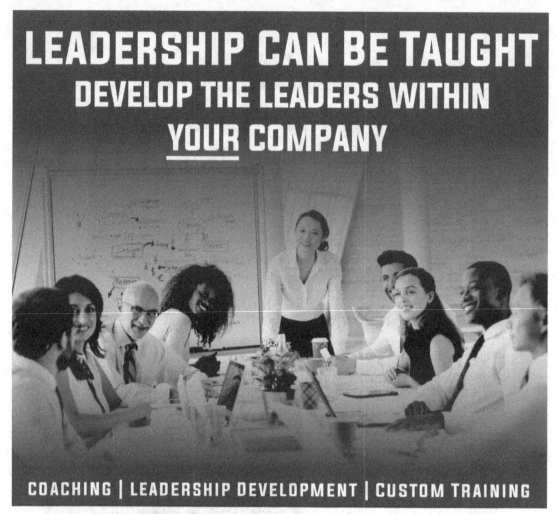